COLIN COWIE
WEDDINGS

TEXT BY JEAN T. BARRETT

LITTLE, BROWN AND COMPANY

BOSTON NEW YORK TORONTO LONDON

Also by Colin Cowie
Effortless Elegance with Colin Cowie

To all the brides who inspire my creativity to make their visions a reality.
—Colin Cowie

First Edition

Library of Congress Cataloging-in-Publication Data

Cowie, Colin.
Weddings / Colin Cowie.
p. cm.
Includes index.
ISBN 0-316-24661-1
1. Weddings—Planning. 2. Wedding etiquette. I. Title.
HQ745.C66 1988
395.2'2—dc21
97-14916

10 9 8 7 6 5 4 3 2 1

Designed by Shahid & Company

RRD–OH
Published simultaneously in Canada by Little, Brown & Company
(Canada) Limited

Printed in the United States of America

CONTENTS

ACKNOWLEDGMENTS

This book has been ten years in the making. It would not have been possible without the help and inspiration of many talented and generous colleagues with whom I have had the pleasure of collaborating.

Thanks go to my agent, Margret McBride, of the McBride Literary Agency, for all her support, and to her associate Winifred Golden; and to my publisher, Little, Brown and Company, in particular editorial director Fredrica Friedman and publisher Sarah Crichton, for their belief in my message.

Writing this book was a pleasurable experience and I have made a wonderful friend in Jean Barrett, a gifted writer who worked diligently to meet all the deadlines. A special thank-you to Lisa Berke for her countless hours of research.

For compiling and sorting through thousands of photographs and for designing this book, a big thank-you to Sam Shahid, Carlos Frederico Farina, and Betty Eng from Shahid & Company. My gratitude also goes to the many photographers whose images appear on these pages and who so magically captured the special moments in this book: Joe Buissink, Jack Caputo, Grey Crawford, Curtis Dahl, Yitzhak Dalal, Alison Duke, Jonathan Farrer, Deborah Feingold, Nadine Froger, Alec Hemer, Beth Herzhaft, Bart Kressa, Judy Lawne, Robin Layton, Brian Miller, Michelle Pattee, Jean-Jacques Pochet, Denis Reggie, Rafael Reisman, Lee Salem, Baron Erik Spafford, Jasper Sky Photography, and Timothy Teague.

Martha Nelson, the managing editor of *InStyle* magazine, has generously enabled me to share many of my weddings with her readers. I am honored to be part of such a successful magazine venture, and to have Martha as a friend.

Many people and companies have been very generous and supportive. I am grateful to Rich Stearns, Robert Hall, and Lisa Carroll Archambault from Lenox Brands; Michael Stern, Cheryl Evanoff, Greg Davis, and Charlie Faerkin from Regal Rents; Ann Diamond from Party Rental Ltd.; Jane Frost from Stamford Tent & Party Rental; Mireille Giuliano from Champagne Veuve Clicquot; and Sarah Powers from Champagne Krug. For the incredible wedding dresses, thanks to Janet Brown and Joe Takashi of Yumi Katsura, and the wonderful people at The Wedding Dress at Saks Fifth Avenue. I am grateful to the talented Shannon McLean of Cose Belle, who made the beautiful wedding dress pictured on page 7, and to Ben at Manolo Blahnik for the gorgeous shoes. For the handsome men's formalwear, thanks to Jonathan Meizler and Germán Valdivia from JonValdi. For the dazzling jewelry, my gratitude also goes to Cynthia Bach of Cynthia Bach Jewelry and to Muffy Potter at Van Cleef & Arpels who showed me how to fashion a tiara from a necklace.

For the gorgeous flowers that have been so beautifully arranged for all these celebrations, thank-you to Walter Hubert of Silver Birches, Elizabeth Ryan of Elizabeth Ryan Floral Designs, Sylvia Tidwell of Sylvia Tidwell Floral Designs, Ron Hudson and Allen Brannigan of Ron Allen Country Flowers, Julio Ticas, and the late Hal Spragg. For the magnificent drapery, thanks to Douglas Johnson of Designs by Douglas. Thanks to Jim Block from Watt's Up Lighting for helping to create such a wonderful ambience at our parties. My gratitude also to chefs Francis Bey, Laurent Marchand, Martin Herold, Claude Segal, and Emeril Lagasse, who prepared the fabulous foods for the brides, grooms, and their guests. The exquisite and delicious cakes, which added the crowning touch to these weddings, were created by Sylvia Weinstock of Sylvia Weinstock Cakes, Linda Goldsheft of The Cake Studio, Jane Lockhart of Sweet Lady Jane, Polly Schoonmaker of Polly's Cakes, Wendy Kromer of Specialty Cakes & Cookies, Donald Wressell, pastry chef at the Four Seasons Hotel in Los Angeles, and Laura Moniz of Laura Moniz Cakes. The gorgeous and creative invitations were designed by Ellen Weldon of Ellen Weldon Design, Marc Friedland of Creative Intelligence, and Marsha Silver of Salutations, Ltd. For musical expertise, thanks to Susan de Bois of de Bois Productions and Stuart White of Steven Scott Productions.

A special thank-you to my dear friend Kenny G, for the creation of "The Wedding Song," which I have used so many times for so many brides, and for the great experience and friendship that came from designing your wedding to Lyndie. Thanks, too, to Jeff and Margo Barbakow for always being such gracious and generous friends.

For their friendship I offer special thanks to Ruth Brandt Spitzer and Frank Bowling. My gratitude also goes to Charles Allen for all the creative inspiration he has given me over the years.

I deeply appreciate the many contributions of my business partner David Berke, who plays a very important behind-the-scenes role in my company. I am forever grateful to my business partner Stuart Brownstein, whose support and vision have been instrumental to my career. Stuart has been the organizer of many of these weddings, and tirelessly helped Jean and me make this book a reality.

Of course, without the brides and grooms, none of this would have been possible. My sincerest thanks to all of you.

Finally, I owe my greatest debt of gratitude to my mother, Gloria, and my late father, Cecil Cowie, who instilled in me a passion for life and inspired me to share my enthusiasm with others.

My business is designing wonderful celebrations. I particularly love designing and arranging weddings. Over the years, I have had the pleasure of helping hundreds of brides create memorable nuptial celebrations—large and small, formal and informal. Together we developed many of the ideas you will discover in this book. I have learned so much from brides and all the talented people involved in our weddings that I am eager to share my stories and advice with you.

I didn't set out to be a wedding designer. When I first moved to Los Angeles, I started a catering business. As it happens, I was hired to cater several weddings. I was able to see, from an inside vantage point, how weddings are produced. And I began to notice the problems. How the bride's dress was too elaborate for the location and time of day. How ordinary the ballrooms looked. How the pace of the evening dragged. How stressful it was for many brides to deal with details on their wedding day. I knew there was a better way to approach this all-important event—a big-picture approach that focused on the tastes, preferences, and personal style of the bride and groom.

A film producer gave me my first opportunity to handle an entire wedding from A to Z. I began by sitting down with the couple and learning everything I could about them—their favorite restaurants, foods, hobbies, colors, fabrics, vacation destinations, and pastimes. I developed a detailed plan for their nuptial celebration, from the rehearsal dinner the evening before to the wedding itself to the farewell brunch the following day. I worked to ensure that every aspect of the celebration, from the bridesmaids' dresses to the icing on the wedding cake, bore the personal stamp of this bride and groom. When the date finally arrived, the weekend celebration flowed seamlessly from one event to the next, culminating in an inspirational wedding ceremony and a fabulous party for 175 guests, with dancing until midnight. After the Sunday brunch, when I had packed the happy newlyweds into their limousine to depart for the airport, I had a moment to relax and think over how all the months of planning had been crowned by an event that the couple would remember fondly for the rest of their lives. "My approach really does work," I remember saying to myself. From then on, I became involved only with weddings where I could work with the couple on every aspect of the celebration to ensure a cohesive, stylish event from start to finish.

I have written this book to inspire you to design a wedding that is completely, utterly yours. Forget what society or tradition dictates about wedding celebrations. I believe there are no rules when it comes to weddings, except one: style should prevail. Style, for me, has nothing to do with the designer clothes you wear, the timepiece on your wrist, or the car that you drive. *True style is a sense of self, a confidence and graciousness that is evident to everyone you come into contact with. It means knowing yourself, what works for you and what doesn't. True style also relates to how we treat one another. It means behaving with consideration and respect toward others. On your wedding day, true style means creating a personal environment to share with the people who are closest to you, and making every single guest as welcome and as comfortable as possible.*

You are about to plan one of the most memorable events of your life. Your wedding is not just another party. This is an opportunity for you

and your fiancé to make a statement of style to your friends and family, old and new, as you embark on your new life together.

This book will show you how to define and express your own personal style, and how to create a celebration that fits you and your fiancé. You'll learn how to design a wedding with a thread of style that weaves through every element—from the invitations, the ceremony, the flowers, the food, the drinks, the music, to the thank-you notes for wedding presents. This book will give you the skills to work with your wedding planner, florist, caterer, dress shop, stationery supplier, and other vendors to create a wedding that is custom-tailored *to you.*

Many brides enter my office feeling overwhelmed by the idea of planning a wedding and feeling uncertain about what they want. Right now, you may feel that way, too. By the time you finish this book, you will be more relaxed and confident about the planning process, and, hopefully, excited about the days and months ahead.

When brides first come to me, they often have a grand celebration in mind. They may feel pressured by assumptions about the proper way to do things and the expectations of family and friends. In response, I always advise stepping back and thinking about the kind of celebration that really feels right—that expresses the interests and desires of *this* bride and her fiancé. There is no rule that says you must serve dinner at your reception or that it must be a formal affair. I often find myself suggesting an alternative approach. A wedding breakfast, with twenty family members and close friends, makes a lovely party after a morning civil ceremony. An afternoon tea served in your backyard is a gracious and innovative way to entertain guests after a daytime wedding service.

As I have made a specialty of designing weddings, people sometimes assume that I do weddings a certain way. Actually, there's no such thing as a Colin Cowie signature wedding. Each one I design is different, because each couple is unique, and the wedding is designed specifically for them. The common thread linking the weddings I have designed is that each reflects the personality and taste of the bride and groom.

Style can prevail even at the most modest of weddings. David Berke, an associate and close personal friend of mine, called me one morning and announced that he and his fiancée, Lisa Blake, were eloping and planned a simple ceremony that very day. Would I and a friend witness the ceremony? Absolutely, I replied, and immediately set about to see how I could make this celebration special. As it happened, I had a huge vase of creamy yellow roses in the living room. I took a bunch of the roses and fashioned a tight nosegay for Lisa. There were enough flowers left to make a boutonniere for David and a wreath for their beloved Portuguese water dog, Tango. An hour after the phone call, I arrived at David and Lisa's home with the flowers. Lisa's bouquet, David's boutonniere, and the whimsical rose collar for Tango helped give the ceremony a personal touch that made it memorable.

While David and Lisa didn't want a conventional wedding, they did want to hold a terrific party at home to celebrate their union. After they returned from their honeymoon, together we planned a cocktail reception. Lisa, a music enthusiast, made several great cocktail party tapes featuring songs by Shirley Horn, Eartha Kitt, and Aretha Franklin, interspersed with 1970s dance music. I went to the flower market, purchased bunches of roses in many colors, arranged them in mismatched vases around the house, and lit about a hundred votive candles. We set up an informal buffet of a few appetizers on the dining room table, passed other hors d'oeuvres on trays, and ended the evening with a delicious wedding cake and a kir royale toast to the happy couple. Everyone had a fabulous time—especially the bride and groom, because the celebration was exactly their style: informal, lively, and fun.

When I meet with a bride to start planning her wedding, I ask a great many questions on a variety of subjects: about her favorite, and least favorite, movies, music, colors, and flowers; her preferences in clothing designers and restaurants; what she'd do if faced with a totally free day during which she could do anything she wished; about her fiancé's tastes and preferences. Based on the answers to the questions, we come up with a concept that is truly a reflection of the bride and groom's personal style.

All the weddings I do are first based on this important information about the bride and groom. The couple's personal style is then woven into every aspect of the wedding—invitations, attire, flowers, menu, china, music. The result is a tasteful wedding that has a consistent style from the very first thing the guests see, the invitations, right through the ceremony, to the reception, the cutting of the cake, and even to the thank-you notes guests receive after having sent a wedding present.

As a bride-to-be, all too quickly you will become involved in the details of planning what for many women is the most important special event of their lives. Before that happens, it is critical to step back and look at your goals for your special wedding day. Start with a clean slate. Because it is your wedding, you can create exactly the sort of day you wish, from start to finish. You don't have to listen to relatives or the dictates of history or tradition. You are changing your role in life, from a single to a married person. This is an opportunity for you and your fiancé to create a celebration that is entirely yours.

Regardless of budget or other constraints, there is no end to how creative you can be in designing your wedding to reflect your personal sense of style and that of your fiancé. Style, creativity, thoughtfulness, organization, and common sense are unrelated to budget, yet are the most important resources you can bring to bear on your wedding plans. Whatever your circumstances, your wedding celebration can be everything you ever dreamed it could be.

At the beginning of your wedding planning process, *don't think small. Think big.* Create the fantasy. You can always scale down later. This approach is far better than starting with just one element, or focusing on small details. A big idea, or a fantasy that captures your imagination, will inspire you and help you create that thread of personal style you'll weave through every element of your own signature wedding.

Perhaps you dream of an outdoor wedding at the weekend cabin in the woods that you and your fiancé are fixing up. Maybe you see yourself being wed in your local community church, surrounded by your family and friends from the congregation. Perhaps your vision is a quick civil ceremony downtown, followed by a chic cocktail reception in a penthouse suite of an elegant hotel. Or maybe you dream of being wed at a favorite winery, surrounded by rows of grapevines, with mountain vistas in the distance.

Designing a wedding comes down to creating that big idea. It is not a matter of going to the florist and looking at her book, asking the caterer to submit menus to you, or asking the band to send you a list of songs. Create the vision of your wedding based on your own personality. Use your imagination to stimulate the creativity of the florist, caterer, or bandleader. Once you have created the big picture, the whole process of dealing with your wedding vendors will go more smoothly because you will have a better idea of what you want. If you don't start with a concept, your wedding may turn into a pastiche of the standard approaches of your various vendors, rather than a celebration that was customized just for you.

As you begin this process, keep my philosophy in mind: I always prefer to do a few things well, rather than trying to do ten things that will stretch my resources. A few elements executed properly is a much more sensible approach than trying to carry off an overly ambitious plan that includes dozens of elements. Wedding celebrations don't have to be elaborate. Two dozen guests invited to partake in a delicious wedding luncheon in the private room of your favorite restaurant, with center-pieces of flowers abundantly stuffed into your collection of colorful Depression glass vases, and a classical guitarist playing background music, makes a delightful celebration that is personal and memorable.

Remember, when you invite guests to share in your nuptials you are inviting them to take a journey with you on one of the most important days of your life. Guests will spend anywhere from a few hours to pos-sibly a few days on this journey with you. You have an opportunity to make your wedding a magical and memorable experience for everyone.

While planning a wedding may seem like a large endeavor, you should enjoy the entire process. Often, it is a once-in-a-lifetime experi-ence. To help you, find creative people who can assist. Enlist your fiancé, friends, and relatives to help you create your special day. Your maid or matron of honor, and your bridesmaids, can be a won-derful source of advice, support, and legwork. Bridesmaids can help you with your invitations, applying ribbon or inserting tissue, stuffing the envelopes and mailing them. They can go to flea markets with you to look for vintage linens or unusual floral containers for your centerpieces. An organized maid or matron of honor can serve as your coordinator on the wedding day itself. Your friends and family want to get involved—think of all the ways that they can make a contribution.

Most of all, on your wedding day, *relax and have fun from start to finish.* Surround yourself with your nearest and dearest friends and relatives to share in your happiness, and make it a celebration that everyone will long remember.

In these pages are hundreds of ideas that have worked for me. I know they will work for you, too. I hope that this book will not only make the process of planning your wedding easier, but also will inspire you to design a wedding that is uniquely yours.

Have fun!

Colin

Erin Malloy and Dutch Edwards, a couple whom I had known for several years, asked for my help in creating an unusual wedding celebration for a group of close friends. Erin and Dutch were adamant that they didn't want a typical "catered affair" in a hotel, club, or restaurant. Their own apartment was too small for the group they had in mind. But in a stroke of good fortune, dear friends had just finalized the purchase of a spacious loft apartment in the heart of the city, which they planned to renovate. Since the space was temporarily empty, they offered it for the celebration. What could be better?

The apartment was only available for a month before the construction crews were to begin work, so Erin and Dutch had to move quickly. They decided to limit the wedding to just twenty-eight of their closest friends. They planned to schedule a party with their families, both of which lived out of state, at a later date.

The apartment had been vacant for several years and needed renovation, but it was an ideal space for entertaining, with a large living/dining room, expansive city views, hardwood floors, and high ceilings. Erin and Dutch both loved the apartment's dilapidated but grand atmosphere and knew it would be perfect for the celebration they envisioned. Tables and chairs could be rented easily and the bride and groom planned to bring over a few furnishings from their home to give the space a lived-in look. Because the reception was for such a small group, we determined that we could use many of the beautiful things that the bride and groom collected, including vintage linens, antique glassware, and a wealth of mismatched fine Lenox china place settings that the bride had inherited from her mother and grandmother.

One feature of the apartment was a massive fireplace with a wooden mantel painted powder blue, a shade Erin loved. We decided to play off that color for many aspects of the wedding celebration. It seemed serendipitous—something borrowed (the apartment), something blue!

The invitations were informal, as befits a gathering of thirty people. A calligrapher friend of Erin's wrote them out in sable ink on heavy powder blue cards bordered in gold. "Dear____, " the invitations read. "We are getting married on Saturday, the third of May and would love for you to share in our celebration. The ceremony will be held at 11 East 68th Street at 7 o'clock in the evening, with an intimate dinner to follow. We hope you can join us. Much love, Erin and Dutch."

Advance preparations were uncomplicated. For the reception dinner, Erin and Dutch envisioned all their guests sitting at one long table, so we rented several rectangular folding tables, along with pads, covering the long table with several mismatched vintage linen and lace cloths. From the florist, we rented a pair of silver trumpet vases, candelabra, and other small containers to hold spring flowers. In several trips the week before the event, Dutch and Erin brought over cartons of things that would be used for the ceremony and reception, including her antique china, three

Top left: Handwritten invitations were evidence of the small size of the gathering. Bottom left: Instead of a ring pillow, a vintage silver box was lined in powder blue card stock. Right: A glittering Van Cleef and Arpels diamond necklace was transformed into a tiara for bride Erin Malloy, who carried a French nosegay of Sterling roses and grape hyacinths, tightly arranged in concentric circles.

dozen vintage linen napkins, and the couple's silver plate service for twelve and two other sets borrowed from friends. The bride and groom combined their collections of vintage and new stemware to make a service for thirty. We purchased dozens of candles to provide an old-world style of lighting for the evening celebration, and dripless tapers for guests to hold during the ceremony.

The groom raided his wine cellar, choosing to serve his guests from his collection of large-format bottles of white and red wines from France, Italy, and California. For the champagne, he decided to sacrifice a jeroboam (the equivalent of four bottles) of Veuve Clicquot, which he had recently won in a sculling race. As he put it, "This is the most special day in my life—what better occasion for this bottle?"

For the final touch, the couple brought over a pair of large, beautifully framed oil paintings of pastoral landscapes that they had recently bought at auction. The antique paintings instantly placed the couple's personal stamp on this long-vacant apartment.

We developed a simple but delicious menu that would be easy to serve from the apartment kitchen and took into account the minimal facilities—a small stove with functioning broiler, a sink, a tiny refrigerator, and almost no food preparation space. Erin and I visited my celebrated cake-baker friend, Sylvia Weinstock, and placed an order for a very special and unusual dessert. We arranged for the apartment to be cleaned on Thursday and had everything but the flowers delivered and set up on Friday, leaving only a few last-minute preparations for the day of the wedding.

The afternoon of the wedding, I cooked at my apartment, ten blocks away, while Erin and Dutch got ready. We taxied over at four P.M., in time to complete the setup. The table had been set the evening before with the mismatched antique plates, stemware, and vintage linens. After an hour's work with the flowers, the apartment looked gorgeous. We filled the trumpet vases with lavish arrangements of delphiniums, bells of Ireland, and mauve hydrangeas. Between the tall arrangements, we placed low, tightly packed containers of Sterling roses, hydrangeas, and table smilax, alternating these with candelabra cascading with roses, smilax, and bunches of green grapes. We placed the candles around the room, set the champagne and the magnums of white wine on ice, and I busied myself with last-minute preparations in the kitchen and briefed the kitchen staff and two waiters. Instead of a sign-in book, we placed a stack of little cards next to a sterling silver box for guests to write messages of felicitation to the bride and groom.

Right at seven P.M., the first guests, including the justice of the peace, arrived. The bridal couple greeted everyone at the door, Erin attired in a powder blue dupioni silk full-length gown with bell sleeves, Dutch in a black crepe suit with a white shirt and powder blue silk tie. Guests—an eclectic group of longtime friends—wore a range of outfits, from casual to elegant, since Erin and Dutch wanted everyone to dress for comfort.

When all had arrived, we assembled and the ceremony began. Erin and Dutch positioned themselves in front of the apartment window as the sun was just beginning to set and the lights of the city were coming on. Their guests stood in an informal semicircle, each holding an unlit candle. The ceremony began with Erin and Dutch together lighting a

Right: The dome-shaped centerpiece echoed the bride's bouquet. Table settings of mismatched crystal, flatware, and china created an effect of insouciant elegance.

Above: Each guest held a single dripless candle during the ceremony.
Right: Shannon McLean, a friend of the bride's, designed and made the bride's wedding gown—and her own maid-of-honor dress.

community candle, then stepping forward and lighting the guests' tapers. Illuminated only by the flickering candles, the justice led the bride and groom through the words of the civil ceremony.

It was a solemn moment—but the solemnity didn't last long. As Dutch kissed his bride, a loud pop could be heard in the background, and a pair of waiters stepped forward holding together the opened jeroboam of champagne. Everyone cheered and quickly looked for a spot to deposit their candles—we had placed several shallow terra-cotta pots filled with sand on the windowsills just for that purpose, so that the candlelight would be reflected in the panes of glass. Soon, each guest was holding a flute of champagne and raising it in a spontaneous toast to the newly-weds. Waiters supplemented the jeroboam with a seemingly endless supply of regular 750-milliliter bottles of Veuve Clicquot, and passed appetizers as guests became acquainted. A strolling violinist provided background music.

After cocktails, the candles on the dining table were lit and Erin and Dutch invited their guests to the table, where pale blue place cards laid out the seating. The first course was the couple's favorite dish from a local bistro, baby frisée (curly lettuce) with a piquant mustard dressing and bits of crisp-fried gammon, or bacon. The rest of the menu was served family-style, with platters set down in the center of the table, to keep the need for servers to a minimum. Baguettes of crusty French bread were placed right on the tablecloth along with shallow dishes of fragrant olive oil for dipping. Guests washed down the salad with magnums of chilled Sancerre, Vernaccia di San Gimignano, and Tocai Friulano, delicious white wines that complemented the dish beautifully.

When the first-course plates had been cleared, the waiters brought out four oversized platters of herb-roasted rack of lamb, garnished with fresh rosemary and set around a mound of roasted new potatoes and a heap of spring vegetables. Bordelaise sauce, brightened with chopped fresh tomato, was set out in a pair of antique gravy boats. As guests helped themselves to the food, waiters brought out magnums of red wine from the groom's collection, including Clos de l'Oratoire 1982 and Meerlust Cabernet Sauvignon 1986, which were placed on the table for guests to sample as they pleased. Between courses, guests stood up to make impromptu toasts. Night having fallen, the long table, lit only with candles and strewn with a still life of delicious food and wine, looked like a medieval banquet scene.

After dinner, the waiters refilled everyone's champagne glass for the traditional toast to the bride and groom with the cutting of the cake. But no grand, oversized cake emerged from the kitchen. Instead, the waiters brought out thirty antique dessert plates, each holding a miniature wedding cake, just right for one generous portion and each decorated to match the pattern of the china. As the cakes were set down in front of each guest, everyone stood up and spontaneously applauded. Dutch's best friend made a touching toast to the bride and groom, who reciprocated with speeches of thanks to their friends for sharing in the celebration.

When the last of the cake had been eaten, the groom stepped over to the stereo, inserted a tape of the couple's favorite 1970s dance music, and turned up the volume to get everyone into the dancing spirit. The upbeat music was interspersed with old standards from the forties, slow dances in a romantic mood. Guests who didn't care to dance stepped over to a small table lit by a candelabra where imported cheeses and decanters of vintage Port, single-malt Scotch, and Armagnac were set out.

Close to midnight, the groom decided everyone needed a bit of fresh air. He enlisted several guests to carry trays of Port and spirits, glasses, a bunch of candles, and a cigar humidor upstairs to the rooftop patio. Earlier in the day, Erin and Dutch had set out several folding chairs and side tables. The evening ended on a reflective note as guests enjoyed quiet chats, mellow cigars, and snifters of Armagnac while the lights of the city sparkled far below.

Left and right: The miniature wedding cakes, created by cake decorator Sylvia Weinstock, amazed the guests.

APPETIZERS
Crudités with Balsamic Vinaigrette

Smoked Salmon Canapés

Champagne Veuve Clicquot Brut

DINNER
Baby Frisée with Mustard Dressing and Crispy Gammon

Magnums of Sancerre, Vernaccia di San Gimignano, and Tocai Friulano

Herb-Roasted Rack of Lamb with a Tomato Bordelaise

Roasted Potatoes, Shallots, and Garlic

Spring Vegetables

Magnums of Clos de l'Oratoire 1982 and Meerlust Cabernet Sauvignon 1986

DESSERT
Individual Chocolate Wedding Cakes

Lemon Cream and Berries

Champagne Veuve Clicquot Brut

Imported Cheeses, Including St. Agur, Montrachet, and Tomme de Savoie

Vintage Port

Coffee

Armagnac

Single-malt Scotch

From the very beginning, actors Vanessa Angel and Rick Otto knew what kind of wedding they wanted. Since her family, who lived in England, and his, from the East Coast, had not yet met, Rick and Vanessa wanted a celebration that was elegant yet informal, providing plenty of opportunities for the families to get to know each other. To keep everything very personal, the couple wanted to limit the ceremony and reception to just sixty guests, their family and closest friends. They preferred a spiritual ceremony rather than a religious one, and Rick planned to recite a poem he had written for Vanessa. Instead of conventional wedding music, they intended to walk down the aisle together to their favorite song by the rock group U2. Wherever their reception would be held, they wanted it to have the intimate, personal ambience of entertaining guests in their own home.

As I thought about how to personalize this celebration, I kept coming back to Vanessa's last name, Angel. When I proposed the use of angels and cherubs as an icon throughout the wedding, both Vanessa and Rick loved the idea.

As the site for this wedding, which was to take place on Easter weekend, we selected a rustic ranch because of its privacy and natural beauty. A grassy knoll between two oak trees provided a dramatic setting for the ceremony. The tennis courts, an easy walk from the ceremony area, were ideally placed for the small reception canopy tent.

The cherub theme was introduced in the wedding invitation package, which was designed using ecru card stock and celery green ink. Embossed with a pair of gold angels at the top, the three-fold invitation packet contained individual cards inviting guests to the rehearsal dinner, wedding, and brunch the following day, plus travel information for out-of-town guests. The cards were tied to each panel of the packet with celery satin and organza ribbon.

In order for the families to get acquainted, a casual party replaced the traditional rehearsal dinner. The bride, groom, and their families gathered in the private dining room of a restaurant conveniently located next to the hotel where they were staying. Everyone was seated at one long table, which was covered with masses of votive candles and small terra-cotta pots stuffed with spring field flowers in vibrant primary colors. The intimate party provided an ideal opportunity to launch the weekend's festivities.

The day of the wedding, Vanessa arranged time for a relaxing massage, manicure and pedicure, and hair and makeup session. At the same time, one crew was installing the reception tent while another was creating an exquisitely overgrown arbor of roses and vines to showcase the ceremony. Behind the tent in the makeshift catering kitchen, the chef and kitchen crew were putting finishing touches on the evening's menu.

As the sun began its late-afternoon descent, guests arrived by vans from their hotel and gathered under a spreading tree for homemade lemonade or sparkling water, refreshing choices on a warm spring afternoon. Guests mingled and admired the dramatic mountain vistas of the ranch while selections from Enya's *Watermark* CD played in the background.

Just before sunset, guests were invited to be seated on natural wood folding chairs arranged in a semicircle beneath the oak trees on either side of a white linen aisle runner. As the little ring bearer made his way

up the aisle followed by the two flower girls, the ceremony began. Dressed in a distinctive black JonValdi tuxedo and wide-lapel satin shirt, worn without a bow tie, Rick crossed the grass, taking his place at the foot of the aisle to await his bride. Enya's mellow vocals segued into the rock group U2's "All I Want Is You."

All eyes were on Vanessa as she stepped into view wearing a stunning form-fitting sleeveless ecru satin gown with a sweetheart neckline and chapel-length train. Her dress was created by John Hayles, the renowned costume designer who designed the dress worn by Marilyn Monroe while standing over the subway grate in *The Seven Year Itch*. Vanessa's long hair was pinned up with a few roses. Carrying a tight nosegay of roses in creamy shades of ivory and white, she walked across the grass to the white aisle runner and joined her groom at the foot of the aisle. Linked arm in arm, the smiling bride and groom walked together to take their vows under an arch covered with a luxuriant arrangement of ivy and roses, backlit so that it glowed with amber light. The brief, simple service was made personal with an exchange of vows that the couple had written, and Rick's recitation of the poem he had written for Vanessa.

As the ceremony concluded, the sun had set, but the full moon and hundreds of thick pillar candles, which were placed in clusters directly on the lawn, illuminated the outdoor cocktail area. A strolling guitarist—a high school friend of the groom's—serenaded guests with classical guitar music as they sampled appetizers and sipped champagne cocktails or sparkling water.

When it was time to dine, guests were directed through a flower-and-vine-wrapped portico into a small tented anteroom. There the three-tiered wedding cake was showcased on a square table covered in taupe damask and strewn with fresh gardenia blossoms and garlands of feathery smilax. The cake, enrobed in white chocolate with its top layer on pedestals, was adorned with frosting swags and tassels and decorated with statuettes of gilded cherubs. Atop the cake, a cherub held a bunch of fresh lily of the valley. An antique chandelier bedecked with candles was hung over the cake to fill the area with soft light.

The band was in full swing as the bride, groom, and guests passed through the anteroom into the canopied dining room. The tent walls were clad in cream-colored upholstered canvas panels, the corners draped with chiffon and hung with gilded cherubs trimmed with cascades of baby ivy and stephanotis blossoms. To increase intimacy, the small tables, set for six and eight guests, were closely spaced. On each table, a gilded cherub held an arrangement overflowing with ivy, hydrangeas, and white Virginia and buttercup yellow roses, set against taupe damask tablecloths. Napkins in the same fabric were tied with gold ribbon. Amber pin spots and votive candles illuminated the floral arrangements. A large crystal and burnished-gold chandelier above the parquet dance floor bathed the area in a golden glow.

Since children were included in the celebration, Vanessa and Rick had engaged a baby-sitter for the whole weekend, allowing parents to relax and have fun. At the reception, the children were seated with their sitter at a special table decorated just for them, where they could enjoy a children's menu and play games.

Overleaf, left: The tented space was kept intimate by using smaller tables and grouping them closely. Pin spots highlight the flowers. Overleaf, right: Formalwear with an edge—the groom's open-necked satin shirt, with a simple boutonniere of lily of the valley.

Because it was Easter weekend, the adults' menu began with a nod to the season—a first course of an eggshell nestled in an eggcup, filled with scrambled egg, topped with caviar, and accompanied by homemade melba toast. A crisp salad was followed by a main course of grilled duck breast. When it was time for the cutting of the wedding cake, a kir royale toast was offered to the couple. After cutting the cake with Vanessa, Rick presented his bride with a sterling silver–framed copy of the poem he had recited during the ceremony. Slices of the vanilla cake were served on an oversized plate with raspberry coulis, spoonfuls of lemon sorbet, and a sprinkling of candied violets. Individual slices were also wrapped in cellophane and placed in little gold cardboard boxes for the guests to take home, an age-old English tradition that delighted Vanessa's family. While background music played during dinner, the meal was served without a break for dancing, a more formal approach to the evening, which gave guests plenty of time for relaxed conversation.

After dinner, the band took the volume up, playing a medley of romantic songs, slow dances, and alternative rock tunes that were favorites of the bride and groom. Guests dined, toasted, laughed together, and danced until it was time for the bride and groom to bid farewell. The following day, the two families and close friends reassembled for a casual Sunday morning brunch around the hotel pool to share experiences about the wonderful weekend they had enjoyed together and to celebrate the new friendships that had been made. A final champagne mimosa toast was made to wish the newlyweds a long and successful life together as they left on their honeymoon.

APPETIZERS
Grilled Shrimp Marinated in Fresh Lime Juice with Feta Cheese and Mint
Asparagus Tips Wrapped in Smoked Salmon and Tied with a Chive
Roederer Estate sparkling wine
Sparkling water

DINNER
Caviar in the Egg with Melba Toast
Salad of Butter Lettuce with Crispy Mushrooms, Crispy Leeks,
and a Chardonnay Vinaigrette
Morgan Chardonnay 1992

Breast of Muscovy Duck with a Bordelaise Grape Sauce
Wild Rice, Carrot Flan
Medley of Vegetables, Including Haricots Verts and Asparagus Tips
Calera Pinot Noir 1991

DESSERT
Vanilla Wedding Cake with White Chocolate Frosting
Served with Raspberry Coulis, Lemon Sorbet, and Candied Violets

Beloved Wife

Thinking of you
on this our special day
all of our dreams
our life together
beginning
walking hand in hand
down the aisle
through the fields of life
towards the mountains
our journey
having begun
as we grow and love
unconditionally
completely
our hearts
now one
loving you Vanessa
my wife
loving you

Rick Otto to Vanessa Angel
April 1996

W hen bride Kai Baker thought about a look for her wedding to her South African fiancé, Doron Linz, she kept coming back to a series of evocative photos she had been saving from the Ralph Lauren Safari fragrance ads. She loved the look of the interiors pictured in the photos, which re-created the feeling of an African safari camp, with billowing, gauzy fabrics draped tentlike from the ceilings. The pictures reminded her of the exciting trip to South Africa when she met her fiancé's family for the first time. When she showed me the images, we immediately saw how we could re-create that colonial feeling at her wedding, which was to be held at a friend's home in midsummer.

While colonial Africa inspired the look of Kai's wedding, the food was to be utterly contemporary and very light, in keeping with her preferences. She wanted the elegant summer buffet menu to offer lots of fish and a veritable cornucopia of delicious fresh vegetables and tropical fruits. Then there was the music. African marimbas would lend an exotic note to the cocktail hour, but later on Kai and Doron wanted to swing to their favorite jazz and Motown music. We had multiple meetings with the bandleader before the song list was finalized to the bride and groom's satisfaction.

At four P.M. on the day of the wedding, the nearby mountains were bathed in blazing afternoon sunshine, but ocean breezes began to cool the intense heat of the day. Guests were beginning to arrive for Kai and Doron's wedding at a hillside estate, loaned for the occasion by friends. Guests assembled on the patio and sipped iced tea under the shelter of large canvas market umbrellas and in the shade of tall, hundred-year-old palm trees. In the center of the courtyard was an expansive pool that, like an oasis in the Serengeti, served as a cooling image in the blazing heat of the afternoon. Gazing at the whitewashed buildings, palms, and lush foliage, and listening to the sounds of exotic African marimba music, guests could easily imagine themselves transported to another time and place.

At first, there was little evidence that a wedding was about to happen. But as the minutes ticked away, lush floral arrangements were brought out from a staging area in the garage, where they had been kept to shelter their delicate blooms from the hot sun. Large urns filled with lavish arrangements of the bride's favorite white flowers—Casablanca lilies, white garden and cabbage roses, and dendrobium orchids—were placed around the ceremony area. The chuppah, or wedding canopy, covered with hundreds of white lilies, roses, and orchids and lavishly draped in swags of tea-stained muslin tied with heavy silk tasseled ropes, was carried into position by eight waiters.

The ceremony began as the groom and his family took their place under the chuppah. Family friend and soprano saxophonist Kenny G played "Silhouette" as Kai made her way from the house, past the pool, and down the aisle to join her husband-to-be. Her gown was an ecru columnar pleated silk Mary McFadden design with a magnificent gold brocade collar. Her hair was pulled back simply, and her bouquet of white roses was loosely gathered, entwined with a trail of gilded bear grass and tied with gold ribbon.

The traditional Jewish ceremony culminated with the rabbi offering the groom a napkin-wrapped glass to break underfoot. As Doron smashed the glass, the fountain in the center of the pool erupted, sending a stream of water high into the air, and the marimba band burst into festive recessional music. Then the bridal couple walked back to the house for a quiet moment together before joining the rest of the wedding party for photographs around the pool.

Meanwhile, guests strolled over to the carpeted tennis courts to enjoy cocktails and hors d'oeuvres under the shelter of large market umbrellas. The marimba band provided lively background music. When the photos were finished, the bride and groom joined their guests for the last few minutes of the cocktail reception before inviting everyone to dine.

The dining tent was draped with gauzy tea-stained muslin tied back with heavy gold silk rope and tassels, perfectly framing the mountain views. Glass bubble vases holding rings of gilded curly willow and packed with garden roses and lilies graced each dinner table. The tables were covered with ivory cloths and lavishly draped with yards of muslin that puddled on the ground. Candelabra infused the tent with warm candlelight.

Oversized floral urns filled with white roses, lilies, and orchids flanked the buffet table, which was accented with a pair of large baroque candelabra. An impressive grilled whole salmon was the buffet's focal

Top left: An elaborately decorated chuppah (wedding canopy) sheltered the wedding party from the heat of the day. Right: The groom is moved by his brother's toast.

point, served with tarragon mayonnaise and side dishes of asparagus and salad, all presented in antique sterling silver serving pieces. The dinner wines were specially imported from Stellenbosch, one of the leading wine regions in South Africa. Later, guests strolled over to an abundant buffet of exotic fruits, including strawberry papayas, pineapple, litchis, passion fruit, long-stemmed strawberries, and mangoes, all arrayed on a muslin-swagged table and illuminated by a heavy sterling silver candelabra. The meal culminated with the cutting of the chocolate and vanilla wedding cake.

After dinner, Kai and Doron took to the dance floor for their first dance, a moving rendition of the Frank Sinatra hit "My Way," played by a ten-piece band with a full horn section. Guests quickly joined the couple on the dance floor, where the sounds of vibrant jazz, rhythm and blues, and Motown dance music kept the evening hopping for hours. Later on, to the delight of all assembled, fellow guest Kenny G joined the band in a spirited jam session, which brought the guests to their feet, clapping and cheering. Late in the evening, when it was time for Kai and Doron to depart, they climbed into a black vintage convertible Mercedes-Benz that awaited them in the driveway, an ideal car from which to wave good-bye to guests. After spending the night at a nearby historic stone inn, the couple departed the next morning on a honeymoon trip to South Africa.

APPETIZERS
Fried Dover Sole with Tartar Sauce
Puff Pastry Triangles with a Mushroom and Chèvre Filling
Neil Ellis Louisvale Chardonnay 1991
Sparkling water

BUFFET
Whole Grilled Norwegian Salmon with Tarragon Mayonnaise
Barbecued Vegetables
Fresh Steamed Asparagus

Insalata Tricolore with Radicchio, Arugula, and Belgian Endive
and a Balsamic Vinaigrette
Kanonkop Pinotage 1990 or Rustenberg Chardonnay 1991

DESSERT
Buffet of Exotic and Tropical Fruit
Chocolate and Vanilla Wedding Cake
Coffee

When I first met with bride Cindy Bozick and her mother, they had all the major elements in place for Cindy's wedding to Andrew Kardish. There would be 350 guests. The ceremony was to be held in the local church that Cindy had attended since she was a child, while the reception would take place at the country club, a centerpiece of the desert resort community where her family had lived for generations. Even the invitations had already been printed.

But Cindy and her mother had some concerns. They were worried about the tight time frame at the church, which wouldn't be available until one P.M. the day of the wedding. Another concern was their country club. Despite the club's refined appointments and the staff's genuine desire to accommodate the bride, the decor was "resort casual," done in a color scheme of mauve and burgundy with sandstone accents, which Cindy didn't like. And while the club offered excellent food, Cindy wanted a more sophisticated menu that would reflect the formality of the reception. Cindy and her mother had also seen a magazine photo of a beautiful bridal bouquet—a single rose composed of dozens of individual rose petals—but no local florist had been able to duplicate it.

When we began to discuss Cindy's favorite things, it was clear that she loved many wedding traditions but wanted to approach her celebration in a new way. She didn't want to be married in a typical white gown, but she did want a full complement of attendants. It was her childhood dream to walk down the aisle to the traditional "Wedding March" from Wagner's *Lohengrin*. She loved creamy off-white colors, but she also adored vibrant corals and dramatic dark greens. An elegant menu of superb food was particularly important to the bride and her family. We also discussed at length how to deal with the many guests who were traveling to the desert from out of town, and the importance of making them feel well taken care of despite the busy schedule of the bride, groom, and their families.

From the beginning, this wedding celebration was designed to be a three-day event. The wedding would be the first time that Cindy's family would meet Andrew's family, from the East Coast. Spreading events throughout the weekend and allowing ample free time would provide family and friends an opportunity to get acquainted. Out-of-town guests could enjoy a weekend getaway in a desert resort community blanketed with golf courses, tennis courts, and swimming pools, and surrounded by dramatic mountains.

The moment guests arrived at their hotel Friday afternoon, they knew they would be specially cared for by the bridal couple. Awaiting each guest was a sumptuous welcome basket, tied with an oversized gold bow and containing a wedding itinerary, a list of local attractions, bottles of mineral water, and an assortment of nuts and fresh desert produce— grapes, oranges, and grapefruit—from the bride's family farm. The itinerary detailed the location of each wedding event and provided explicit travel directions. The guide to local attractions covered every-thing from a remarkably beautiful hiking trail to recommendations of the best salons for a facial and massage. A personal note from Cindy and Andrew expressed their gratitude for each guest's attendance, and hinted at the pleasures to come.

Top left: The cocktail reception tables looked out upon the golf course, with mountains in the background.

The ceremony was to be held at the Bozick family's community church, a vast, cathedral-like contemporary structure. As a member of the church, Cindy was respectful about conforming to parish regulations on decorations and the timing of installations. Morning services ended at one o'clock and the wedding was scheduled for three, leaving little time for decorating. The challenge was to create a warm, intimate atmosphere in a vast, impressive setting—and do it on a deadline.

The country club also had to be transformed. The color of the ballroom floor was easily changed; a rental company placed a temporary overlay of ivory carpeting on top of the existing mauve carpet. Inside the room, padded ecru-colored wall panels covered mauve walls. But the ballroom entrance was awkwardly situated so that guests entered the room from the side, rather than making a formal central entrance. So a new ballroom entrance was created. Ivory chiffon was wrapped over a simple tent frame from a local rental company, creating a tunnel that redirected guests into the ballroom through what was previously a side exit. With the new layout, guests could make a grand entrance into the center of the room from the patio overlooking the golf course, and immediately respond to the beauty and elegance of the space.

Creating the sophisticated menu that Cindy and her family wanted required weeks of working closely with the club's food and beverage department. An agreement was reached to use a guest chef who would coordinate with the club's executive chef to create a menu and oversee the food service. Specialty foods, such as caviar and smoked salmon, as well as fine wines and spirits, would be brought in for the occasion.

On the day of the wedding, preparations went into high gear. Precisely at one P.M., the crew at the church, which had preassembled most of the floral arrangements in an anteroom, began the installation. Potted trees were placed to block off unused portions of the sanctuary, creating a more intimate setting. An enormous, preassembled archway woven of white French lilac, Queen Anne's lace, and pale yellow Message, orange Sensation, and ivory Porcelana roses was set at the foot of the aisle to create a magnificent visual focal point and frame the bride's entrance. The pews were swagged with ivory chiffon to prevent unwanted foot traffic, and the aisle was lined with a crisp white runner. Pew posts were decorated alternately with hurricane candles and masses of creamy roses. A simple garden urn, covered with moss and filled with flowers, greeted the guests as they entered the church vestibule. Flats of white impatiens brightened the garden planters just outside.

Everything came together with great effect and on time, bringing Cindy's dream of her special wedding ceremony to life. "The most important design element was the feeling of intimacy created at the church and carried through to the reception," Cindy says. "Having a large wedding, I didn't want to lose sight of the reason that we were doing all of this, which was my marriage to Andrew."

As the minutes ticked off before the guests arrived at the church, Cindy and her bridesmaids were ensconced in a separate room, finishing their preparations for the service and laughing as they reminisced about the rehearsal dinner. Held at a casual Italian restaurant, it proved a comfortable place for the large party of family and local and out-of-town friends to become better acquainted.

Left: The bridal party's bouquets were created with dozens of creamy white Virginia rose petals glued together to form a single oversized camellia-like flower.

Guests entered the church to the sound of hymns sung by the thirty-member boys' choir attired in red robes. With the opening strains of Pachelbel's Canon in D Minor, the ceremony began. First to enter were the bride and groom's grandmothers, who were seated in the front row. The parents entered next, followed by the groom, best man, and minister. The four bridesmaids and four groomsmen followed and took their place at the altar; then there was a dramatic pause. Wrapped in a strapless bodice and pencil skirt of silk charmeuse in soft peach, with full-length gloves and a short veil trimmed in matching silk, Cindy walked down the aisle to the traditional "Wedding March" from *Lohengrin*. She carried the bouquet she had dreamed of: a simple but dramatic bloom composed of dozens of creamy white Virginia rose petals glued together to form a single oversized camellia-like flower, which had been created by my most talented florist. The service was filled with music, songs, prayers, and readings given by family members and friends. Newlyweds Cindy and Andrew walked down the aisle together to joyous recessional music, and waited in a church anteroom for photos to be taken with the wedding party.

Meanwhile, guests headed to the reception at the country club. As guests entered the club lobby, the classical consort that had performed early in the ceremony was playing. The cocktail reception was held on the club patio, where guests were greeted by waiters in white dinner jackets passing trays of hors d'oeuvres and glasses of champagne. The abundance of bubbly, and of caviar on melba toast, spicy shrimp, lamb loin, smoked salmon on puff pastry, and baby potatoes stuffed with ratatouille, swept guests immediately into the spirit of celebration. As the reception continued, a jazz ensemble kicked up the beat. Cocktails and sparkling water were served from two bars as everyone mingled.

After a short photo session on the greens of the golf course, the bridal party arrived and the cocktail hour segued into dinner as guests were escorted into the ballroom, transformed into an elegant setting with ivory walls and carpeting and voluminous draping of ivory chiffon around the stage. Oversized ivory rosettes made of dozens of individual rose petals, evoking Cindy's bridal bouquet, were used as tiebacks for the chiffon draping. A fourteen-piece big band played standards from the thirties and forties.

The dining tables were covered with heavy French floral damask cloths in taupe with ecru accents. Gilded chairs complemented the gold flatware set beside heavy glass charger plates dotted around the rim with dramatic raised gold teardrops. Oversized white Irish linen napkins were tied with two-and-a-half-inch wired gold bows that recalled the bows that had crowned guests' welcome baskets. The focal point at each table was a free-form rose topiary centerpiece abundantly studded with white French lilac, Queen Anne's lace, and full-blown roses in the same pale yellow, ivory, and orange color palette used in the ceremony.

Making a grand entrance to a round of applause, Cindy and Andrew launched the evening's festivities. The elegant sit-down dinner began with ravioli filled with wild mushrooms in a light veal stock sauce as first course, followed by a salad of butter lettuce, arugula, and crispy leeks, served with a rich chardonnay. The main course, filet of beef with a rosemary tomato coulis, sautéed baby red potatoes, asparagus tips, baby carrots, and a variety of other fresh vegetables, was accompanied by a

Pin-spot lighting illuminated the towering floral arrangements on the tables, while subdued ambient lighting created an intimate atmosphere in the room.

vintage Bordeaux. An alternative of roasted whitefish with a light tomato sauce was offered as well. After dinner, an assortment of vintage Ports, imported cheeses, figs, and crusty French bread was arranged on a buffet station.

At the peak of the evening, Cindy and Andrew cut the wedding cake. The cake was simple yet dazzling: four hexagonal tiers with sheets of white chocolate draped over each layer, decorated with an abstract floral motif and teardrops of gold that matched the design of the glass charger plates. In addition to the cake, the dessert assortment included ice cream in an almond tuile, a mini crème brûlée, and berries with a sprig of mint.

After dinner, the bride and groom joined their guests on the dance floor. During the father-daughter dance to "Sunrise Sunset," Cindy's energetic father caused a sensation with his ballroom dancing moves as he twirled and spun the bride. Cindy recalls her father's capers as one of her most cherished memories of the day.

A casual Sunday brunch, hosted by Cindy's parents at their home, ended the weekend on a relaxing note. Flowers from the wedding and reception were enjoyed again. Faded stems were simply replaced with fresh blooms. The brunch, served buffet-style in the kitchen, featured fresh fruit salad, croissants, and smoked salmon, along with omelettes made to order. Guests were offered a variety of fresh juices or mimosas. Attended by forty guests, the brunch provided a time to recall the joyous events of the past few days. The timing allowed out-of-town guests a chance to say their good-byes, while Cindy and Andrew, whose honeymoon departure was not scheduled until the next day, had the balance of the day to open their gifts and reminisce about this wonderful wedding with their family and close friends.

APPETIZERS

Smoked Salmon on Puff Pastry

Spicy Shrimp

Caviar on Melba Toast

Lamb Loin with Onion Marmalade

Baby Potatoes with Ratatouille

BEVERAGES

Champagne Veuve Clicquot

Red and white wine

Frozen vodka in ice molds

Sparkling and still mineral water

DINNER

Ravioli Filled with Wild Mushrooms in a Light Veal Stock Sauce

with Sautéed Mushrooms, Diced Tomato, and Fresh Herbs

Grgich Hills Chardonnay 1992

Salad of Butter Lettuce and Arugula with Crispy Leeks

Filet Mignon with a Rosemary Tomato Coulis

Sautéed Baby Red Potatoes

Medley of Asparagus Tips, Baby Carrots, Green Peas, Haricots Verts,

Carved Zucchini, and Baby Turnips

Château Bon Pasteur 1990

or

Roasted Whitefish with a Light Tomato Sauce

Served Over a Confit of Onions and Lentils

Grgich Hills Chardonnay 1992

CHEESE AND PORT STATION

Stilton, Montrachet, and St. André

Fresh Figs

Crusty French Bread

Vintage Port

DESSERT

Vanilla Wedding Cake

Ice Cream in an Almond Tuile

Mini Crème Brûlée

Raspberry Coulis

Fresh Raspberries and Sprigs of Mint

Demitasse coffee

K athy Kaehler and Billy Koch, who are both personal fitness trainers, did not want a typical frills-and-bows wedding. They told me they saw themselves being married in a dramatic setting that would reflect their love of the outdoors. They preferred simple wildflowers to elaborate floral arrangements, and casual style to formality. I was delighted to learn that Kathy never missed a flea market and enjoyed hunting for antiques everywhere from garage sales to fashionable shops. She had amassed quite a collection of 1950s tablecloths and linens, vintage serving pieces, candlesticks and candelabra, and even vintage luggage.

I immediately saw how we could expand on Kathy's collections to create a truly unforgettable country atmosphere at her wedding. For months, she and I had fun scouring flea markets, picking up vintage linens and silver plate creamers, sugar bowls, pitchers, and ice buckets at bargain prices. We incorporated these pieces into unique table settings and buffet arrangements at the reception.

Kathy and Billy also wanted a special look for the wedding party attire. Kathy picked out her wedding dress, an understated white gown that fit the outdoor setting. For the bridesmaids, we had pretty garden-party dresses made in cotton fabric covered with a retro print of bright red cherries. We took all the groomsmen shopping and found crisp sage linen suits and white shirts. The groomsmen paid for their new summer suits, while Billy gave each man the shirt and a different Armani tie in coordinating colors. Billy's three-piece suit was custom-tailored of sage linen. The result was a crisp, classic look for the wedding party that was exactly what the bride and groom had in mind.

As they drove up the long, dusty dirt road leading to a rustic ranch in the mountains, guests must have wondered what kind of wedding they were about to witness. But after they parked and started walking to the gate leading to the ranch, they saw a welcoming antique cast-iron tub filled to the brim with masses of colorful wildflowers, including huge, bright yellow sunflowers. Under a shady tree, a waiter stood offering a tray of glasses filled with a refreshing mixture of lemonade and iced tea garnished with a sprig of fresh mint.

When everyone had gathered, guests walked up a meandering garden path and were seated in the round on chairs arranged under the canopy of an ancient oak. The branches of the tree were hung with rusted wire baskets lined with moss and filled with more wildflowers in every hue, and ivy cascading over the sides. The ceremony began with the music of a flute as the bridal party made its way down the winding path. First came the parents, then the groom and his linen-suited groomsmen, followed by the bridesmaids, carrying hand-tied bouquets of fresh garden flowers.

After the attendants had taken their seats, Kathy made her entrance on the arm of her father. She wore a white silk gown with short lace sleeves, a brocade bodice, and a scoop neckline, and over her head was a simple, chapel-length veil of white tulle. Kathy's bouquet was a traditional arrangement of garden roses in bright colors. She wove her way between the rows of guests, who were seated in a three-quarter circle, and joined Billy under the spreading canopy of the tree for an interfaith ceremony, with both a minister and rabbi officiating.

When the ceremony was over, the newlyweds joined their guests for champagne cocktails, mineral water, and appetizers as Frank Sinatra recordings and jazzy standards, favorites of the bride's, played in the

background. The bar was outfitted with an amusing collection of mismatched vintage colored tumblers—another flea-market find. Bottles of wine, champagne, and sparkling water were arranged in a big zinc tub full of ice that was placed on a side table. Guests mingled by the ranch pool, which looked like a rustic farm pond, surrounded by river boulders and ferns.

After proceeding through an informal receiving line in which they were greeted by the bride and groom's parents, guests reached the seating display, set on an easel. Replacing the traditional host cards, the seating chart showed the arrangement of tables in the dinner tent. A floral arch of ferns, lavender, lilac, and Queen Anne's lace marked the entrance to the tent. The lively sounds of the four-piece band drew guests inside, where the vintage country wedding theme came to life.

To convey the atmosphere of a country market, the natural grass of the field was used as a carpet and the tent ceiling was hung with bunches of dried flowers and gypsophila (baby's breath), and baskets filled with newspapers, flowers, and baguettes of bread. No two tables were dressed alike. Each was arrayed in a different vintage floral-print tablecloth draped over calico cotton underskirts, which had been stained with tea to give them the patina of age. As centerpieces, a variety of mismatched antique silver plate coffeepots, sugars and creamers, water pitchers, and ice buckets were abundantly stuffed with garden roses and fresh herbs, including lavender, parsley, rosemary, and thyme. After the wedding, the centerpieces and linens were incorporated into Kathy and Billy's home, already decorated in a vintage country motif.

For dinner as the sun was setting, a sumptuous but casual buffet was designed. The first course, a hearty vegetable soup with a dollop of garlicky pistou (pesto) sauce, was served in a hollowed-out *boule* (a round loaf of bread) at the tables. The rest of the meal was presented buffet-style in oversized gleaming copper casseroles. The buffet tables resembled a well-stocked flower market, with bundles of gypsophila, Queen Anne's lace, sunflowers, and other blooms stuffed separately into a variety of mismatched containers, including galvanized tin watering cans and buckets. Rustic wrought-iron candelabra from Kathy and Billy's collections held candles that illuminated the buffets.

When dinner was over, Kathy and Billy led off the dancing to "Proud Mary," and guests soon joined them on the dance floor to rock to the couple's favorite hits. After a round of toasts and speeches, the couple cut their wedding cake. Covered with white chocolate frosting and adorned with fresh flowers, the chocolate cake was served with an apricot coulis and fresh berries.

After the final dance set, the honking of a car horn drew the celebrants outside. There, a mint-condition white vintage Mercedes convertible awaited to whisk the bridal couple away. Guests cheered and applauded as the couple climbed into the sleek roadster. As Kathy tossed her bouquet into the delighted crowd, the car pulled out into the narrow dirt road, and the couple was off on their honeymoon and a sparkling new life together.

Left: The cherry-print cotton and crisp linen suits of the bridal party's attire spelled summer in the country. Right: The bride and groom participate in the traditional Jewish hora (a boisterous wedding dance).

APPETIZERS

Smoked Trout on Rounds of Rye

Baby Potatoes Filled with Crème Fraîche and Caviar

Spicy Shrimp

Vegetable Strudel

Champagne cocktails

Sparkling water

DINNER

First Course

Country Pistou Soup Served in a Bread Boule

Baker's Basket of Crusty Breads, Fragrant Olive Oil, and Olive Tapenade

Bonny Doon Vineyards Vin Gris de Cigare 1992

Buffet

Barbecued Spring Lamb Kabobs on Rosemary Skewers with a Mint Pesto

Barbecued Marinated Chicken Skewers

Saffron and Wild Rice

Grilled Chopped Vegetable Salad—Japanese Eggplant, Zucchini, Bell Peppers,

Belgian Endive, and Scallions

Salad of Mixed Baby Greens with a Chardonnay Dressing

Clos du Bois Merlot 1992

Simi Chardonnay 1993

DESSERT

Chocolate Wedding Cake with White Chocolate Frosting

Served with Fresh Berries and Apricot Coulis

Iron Horse Vineyards Wedding Cuvée Sparkling Wine

Actress Holly Robinson was bursting with ideas when I met with her to talk about her wedding to professional quarterback Rodney Peete. She planned to have 325 guests for an early-evening summer wedding—a "somewhat serious ceremony" followed by an "all-out great party." For her reception dinner, Holly knew exactly the kind of menu she did *not* want: fancy food, what she jokingly termed "chicken stuffed with à-la-something!" She expressed her love of down-home Southern dishes, presented in an informal manner, with chefs cooking in front of the guests. In short, she and her husband-to-be favored fun over pomp and circumstance.

But Holly was also a romantic at heart. Since childhood, she'd had a vision of being married in a fairy-tale dress with a full skirt, billows of tulle, and lots of sparkles. She saw herself in an evening setting with twinkling lights. Other "musts" on Holly's list included a sign-in book in a romantic gazebo, showers of rose petals, and hundreds and hundreds of gorgeous roses—"roses everywhere!"

A contemporary private home, loaned for the occasion by family friends, provided a wedding setting that was comfortable and relaxed, and lent itself to the romantic, fairy-tale ambience Holly wanted for her celebration. Spacious gardens were ideal for a cocktail reception while the privacy of the estate assured celebrity guests of a worry-free atmosphere. A cantilevered tennis court with panoramic views made an ideal setting for a night of dinner and dancing under the stars. At the same time, working in a private home required extra care to respect the owner's property. Workers entering the house wore surgical booties over their shoes at all times.

Original plans had been to hold the ceremony in the back garden, but a last-minute switch had to be made when it was realized that the owner, hoping to make the grounds more beautiful for Holly and Rodney's big event, had planted a cascading flower garden and added a fountain that left too little room for the ceremony. Switching the ceremony site to the front garden, with the facade of the house and front porch as the backdrop, actually enhanced the feeling of fairy-tale romance. Decorated with garlands of roses and vines and accented by four standing candelabra adorned with soft pink and lavender roses, the porch provided the perfect backdrop for the ceremony.

The event began at six P.M., when the first guests made their way up the driveway to the pre-ceremony area, where they were greeted by waiters with trays of sparkling water and Rose's lime juice. From a balcony above the porch, a classical string quartet played Handel's *Water Music* suite. White wooden chairs for 325 guests spanned the front yard. A gazebo of white wrought iron, capped with white tulle and clusters of pink roses, housed the guest book.

The groom and his ushers waited in the living room, which they shared with the Reverend Jesse Jackson, a friend of the family, who would officiate at the ceremony. In a private tent at the end of the long cobblestone driveway the bride awaited the music to announce her grand entrance. The tent, erected specifically for that purpose, was outfitted with chairs, a big fan to ward off the summer heat, and mirrors

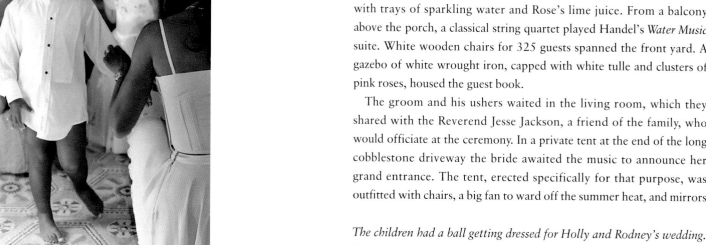

The children had a ball getting dressed for Holly and Rodney's wedding. The high spirits of the kids helped ease any last-minute tensions.

and lighting to facilitate last-minute freshening of hair and makeup.

As the bridal party prepared for the procession, Rodney, inspired by the moment, wrote his bride-to-be a short note expressing his feelings of love and commitment, and had it hand-delivered by the best man. In her dressing room, Holly could not hold back the tears as she read the note. "It was the sweetest thing I have ever read," she recalls.

When guests had all been seated, a pair of ushers walked down the aisle, unfurling a white aisle runner that was bracketed by two nosegays of roses. To the lilting sounds of Handel's "Air" from the *Water Music* suite, seven bridesmaids, beautifully attired in long, off-the-shoulder rose quartz crepe organza dresses, walked down the aisle to the porch. They were followed by the proud, though nervous, junior bridesmaid. Magic Johnson's young son, who served as ring bearer, was initially reluctant to walk down the aisle among so many people. But when his father whispered that Rodney had a whole bunch of his favorite candy in his pocket, the little boy walked gamely down the aisle to get his reward, which brought smiles to the crowd.

To Kenny G's "Wedding Song," the flower girls preceded Holly and her parents down the aisle. Holly wore a snow white Richard Glasgow gown with a form-fitting bodice and a full skirt of pleated tulle, studded with diamond rhinestones that sparkled in the twilight. As she took her place next to the groom, a vocalist sang the Lord's Prayer from the balcony above. Then, after the Reverend Jesse Jackson had warmed up the audience with congenial remarks and more than a few jokes, the couple recited their vows.

As Rodney was invited to kiss his bride, a profusion of rose petals was tossed from the balcony over the bride, groom, and wedding party.

Then, like thunder, the unmistakable sound of drums was heard as the full marching band of the University of Southern California—Rodney's alma mater—paraded up the aisle trumpeting a stirring martial tune. As the band marched in precise pairs up the aisle to the bride and groom, then split into two lines, complete astonishment was evident on Rodney's face, until he realized his fun-loving bride was responsible for this special surprise. With the USC fight song as their recessional, the laughing bride and groom followed the band out of the ceremony area.

Picking up where the marching band left off, singer Charlie Jené and her energetic rhythm and blues band enticed guests into the back garden for the cocktail reception. Formally attired waiters passed trays of hors d'oeuvres as the guests mingled. Champagne was poured from impressive oversized Methuselahs (each the equivalent of eight bottles), to the delight of the guests.

When it was time for dinner, the strains of mellow music spun by a DJ drew guests over to the tennis court. Waiters gave each couple or single guest a miniature scrolled silver picture frame, engraved with "Holly and Rodney" and the wedding date, and holding a calligraphied card with the guest's name and table number. After the wedding, Holly and Rodney sent guests a small wedding photo to place in the keepsake frames.

The tennis court had been transformed into a romantic space for dining and dancing. At night, the wire mesh fencing that enclosed the court became invisible, while providing the perfect framework to drape strings of fairy lights, framing the view of the city lights below. Guests felt as though they were standing on top of the world! When the bridal party entered the reception, dancing began immediately and a great party was under way. Mr. and Mrs. Rodney Peete were introduced and

Left: Once the sun had set, the chain-link fence surrounding the tennis court disappeared into darkness and the fairy lights defined the space. Strategically placed heaters ensured the guests' comfort.

took to the dance floor, amid applause, for their first dance as a married couple, to L.T.D.'s "Love Ballad."

The dinner tables, covered in ivory floral damask, with formal silver place settings and fine crystal stemware, reflected the romance of the occasion. Tucked into each brocade-edged dinner napkin was a hand-scripted menu in elegant calligraphy. Centerpieces of gilded urns filled with ivory Porcelana, pale yellow Message, lavender Sterling, and pale beige Abraham Derby roses were accented with gilded peppercorns and seeded eucalyptus. Canopies of white tulle, hung with fairy lights, were placed over the bridal table and the dance floor.

Three kitchens, each serving a separate buffet station, offered a feast of "foods you want to eat," remembers Holly. The theme was down-home Southern cooking, with California-style gourmet thin-crust pizzas adding a contemporary touch. One station offered deep-fried catfish, cooked to order in huge woks in front of the guests and served with savory rice. Another served deep-fried chicken, black-eyed peas, collard greens, and corn bread. The final station offered an array of thin-crust pizzas, with six chefs preparing combinations of topping ingredients, such as shrimp with pesto sauce and barbecued chicken with fresh corn. After the Reverend Jesse Jackson blessed the meal, the guests began to dine.

The evening was filled with rounds of toasts offered for the bride and groom. The couple reciprocated with their own speech after cutting the cake. Five double layers high, designed to look like an elegant garden gazebo laden with flowers, the confection fulfilled Holly's dream of a fairy-tale wedding cake, although, she says with a laugh, "only Magic Johnson got a really good look at the top, it was so tall."

After the bouquet toss came wild cheers for the garter toss. As Rodney reached under Holly's billowing skirt, he kept pulling out trick items she had planned for him to find—his supposed "little black book" from bachelor days, a pair of tiny dolls (symbolizing babies)—each item greeted with gales of laughter from the guests. Finally, Rodney waved the garter overhead triumphantly and, to much applause, flung it to the waiting bachelors. The evening came to a grand finale as the couple climbed into their getaway car, a vintage Rolls-Royce, complete with driver in traditional footman garb, while guests threw rose petals and shouted farewell wishes.

Top left: The dining area at the magical moment of twilight, just before guests were ushered in.

APPETIZERS
Spicy Cajun Shrimp Skewers
Corn and Crab Cakes
Baby Potatoes Filled with Baba Ghanoush
Tangy Lamb Kebabs with Cumin and Yogurt Sauce
Champagne Veuve Clicquot Brut in Methuselahs
Sonoma-Cutrer Chardonnay 1993
Joseph Phelps Cabernet Sauvignon 1991
Sparkling water

BUFFET DINNER
The Catfish Kitchen
Deep-Fried Catfish Cooked to Order, Served with Ponzu Sauce
Spanish Savory Rice
Salad of Greens with a Tangy Citrus Dressing
Hush Puppies

The Southern Fried Chicken Kitchen
Southern Fried Chicken
Mashed Potatoes and Gravy
Black-eyed Peas
Collard Greens
Corn on the Cob
Corn Bread

The Pizza Kitchen
California Thin-Crust Pizzas to Order with Choice of Shrimp Pesto,
Barbecued Chicken and Corn, Tomato and Basil,
or Barbecued Vegetable
Talbott Vineyards Chardonnay 1993 or
Beringer Vineyards Private Reserve Cabernet Sauvignon 1990

DESSERT
Lemon Wedding Cake, Served with a Fresh Rasperry Sauce
Champagne Veuve Clicquot Demi-Sec

F rom the outset, Elisa Rush and her mother wanted a very contemporary concept for Elisa's wedding. Both Elisa and her parents live in modern homes and favor simple design and clean lines. They also knew exactly where they wanted to hold the wedding: the ballroom of their favorite hotel, a romantic Mediterranean-style establishment tucked into a wooded canyon. But the ballroom was decorated in a garden motif, which did not suit their taste.

And while the family favored modern style, they also wanted a traditional Jewish ceremony that incorporated many rituals highlighting the importance of family and religious heritage.

Since Elisa and her husband-to-be, Jeff, are passionate about fine food and wine, the food and wine had to be exceptional, and since the couple adore great Motown and rhythm and blues music, they wanted their reception to feature a talented band for dancing. Finally, a cigar bar was a must!

At seven P.M. on a Saturday in February, friends, family members, and busi-ness colleagues gathered for Elisa and Jeff's black-tie wedding. With a chamber orchestra playing "Sunrise Sunset," the wedding began in the hotel ballroom, although not a trace of the room's original decor could be seen.

Instead, the room had been transformed into a contemporary, clean white space. White fabric was stretched over pipe frames, hiding apricot wall coverings; peach curtains were replaced with white, and white carpet was laid over the existing floral print. White chairs neatly arranged before a white chuppah completed this minimalist canvas. Two white columns adorned with dramatic arrangements of calla lilies, their tall, slender stems adding height and majesty, bracketed the aisle. The white-on-white color scheme was chosen because the simple decor elements required a clean, uncluttered backdrop for dramatic effect.

Out-of-town guests staying at the hotel had been presented with a welcoming note from the bride and groom along with a scented candle nestled in a white box and tied with white ribbon, a hint of the evening's contemporary look and color scheme.

For this traditional Jewish ceremony, male guests were offered white yarmulkes. As the processional "Dodi Li" began, four generations of the two families walked down the aisle. Grandparents took their seats, and the groom's parents and immediate family on both sides stood under the chuppah to bear witness. Adding to the symbolism, Elisa's grandfather's tallis (prayer shawl) was used to form the chuppah canopy. It was placed between two lengths of sheer white chiffon, supported by poles adorned with sprays of gypsophila. Behind the chuppah, the picture window of the ballroom showcased a large planter that had been replanted with calla lilies.

The traditional Jewish song "Erev Shel Shoshanim" announced the bride. Preceded by her two young nieces, and on the arm of both proud parents, Elisa wore a simple A-line silk-twill gown designed by Yumi Katsura, and carried a perfectly round nosegay of creamy stephanotis blossoms. A traditional Jewish service, with readings and songs, united the couple. After the glass had been broken and the kiss shared, the family filed back down the aisle to the joyful "Mazel Tov."

Top: A pair of swans, full-time residents at the hotel where the Rush-Port wedding was held.

Top left: The crew works on transforming the ballroom with white cotton draping, white carpeting, and white calla lilies. Middle left: All the tables were preset, allowing for a quick and easy changeover during cocktails.

Top left: Part of the ballroom was used for the ceremony. Bottom left: While guests enjoyed cocktails on the patio, the ballroom was magically transformed from ceremony space to dining room. Top right: Groomsmen carry in the chuppah to signal the beginning of the ceremony. Bottom: The groom is hoisted aloft in the traditional hora.

A jazz combo began to play on the adjoining outdoor terrace, where guests assembled to enjoy cocktails and hors d'oeuvres. As the newly-weds mingled, greeting guests, another transformation was quietly under way. The hotel ballroom was changing yet again, from synagogue to dining room.

Wall panels of white fabric, which had been specifically set in place to create an intimate ceremony area, hid more than wallpaper. Behind the false wall were a dozen completely set dinner tables. With only forty-five minutes (the duration of the cocktail hour) to change over the room, the crew moved swiftly, moving the tables, placing white slipcovers over the chairs, which had been used just moments before at the service, and arranging them around the tables. Onstage, the band replaced the chuppah. The portion of white carpet that concealed the dance floor was removed and wall panels were rearranged. With the light level adjusted, candles lit, pin-spot lighting appropriately directed, and the band playing, the room was ready for the guests to reenter.

Keeping to the white-on-white theme, tables were dressed in white cotton twill and set in a contemporary manner with plain silver and crystal. Centerpieces were masses of gypsophila, held in low silver rounds, alternating with tall silver candelabra filled with cascading clouds of that same tiny white flower. The room was softly lit in pink and amber hues, ensuring that so much white would not seem stark or cold.

As guests reentered the ballroom, Elisa and Jeff stepped to the dance floor for their first dance, which segued into the "Hora," with guests joining together to lift the newlyweds high into the air in the traditional dance. Then the atmosphere turned spiritual as everyone took their seats and the eldest members of the families offered a prayer for the couple and blessed the challah (bread). The challah was then shared with guests, each portion signifying that person's approval.

Since fine food and wine are among Jeff and Elisa's greatest pleasures, dinner was a formal affair. A four-course menu featured a porcini mushroom ravioli first course provided by Elisa's sister, who owns a gourmet pasta company. A simple salad of arugula and butter lettuce was topped with crisp-fried leeks. After a brief session of dancing, guests enjoyed a main course of rack of lamb with a tomato Bordelaise sauce, baby potatoes, and vegetables.

After dinner had been served, festivities resumed with the father-daughter dance. Those who preferred dining to dancing visited the cheese station, sampling imported English and French cheeses, fresh figs, and walnut-raisin bread. The feast culminated with a dessert medley and slices of a spectacular wedding cake. The sleek four-layer cake, with the top layer on a pedestal over a cluster of pastillage calla lilies, was enrobed in creamy white rolled fondant with translucent white silk ribbon around the bottom of each layer. Capping the festivities, vintage Port was served at the cheese station, and a humidor stocked with premium cigars was brought around to the guests.

At the end of the evening, the bride and groom said their good-byes and retreated to their honeymoon suite in the hotel. To their surprise and delight, the private spa tub in their suite bubbled away. Romantic music was playing on the stereo; dozens of votive candles arranged around the suite burned softly; champagne was chilling on ice; hundreds of rose petals thickly covered the bed. A disposable camera was placed on a side table to capture the scene and the moment. It was a magical ending to a magical wedding, the day they would treasure.

APPETIZERS

Caviar with Toast Points or Blini

Chilled Asparagus with Truffle Dressing

Smoked Salmon Sliced to Order

Dom Ruinart Blanc de Blancs Champagne

Sparkling water

DINNER

Porcini Mushroom Ravioli in a Veal Stock Sauce

Domaine Drouhin Pinot Noir 1992

Salad of Butter Lettuce, Arugula, and Crispy Leeks

Rack of Lamb with a Tomato Bordelaise Sauce

Baby Red Potatoes

Medley of Haricots Verts, Green Peas, and Spring Carrots

Opus One 1991

IMPORTED CHEESE SERVICE

Stilton, Chèvre, and St. André

Figs and Walnut-Raisin Bread

Vintage Port

DESSERT

Wedding Cake Served with Raspberry Coulis, Fresh Berries, and Mint

Mini Crème Brûlée

Homemade Lavender Ice Cream in an Almond Tuile

Champagne Billecart-Salmon Rosé 1990

B ride Tamara Hughes had grand plans for her wedding to Eric Gustavson. She wanted a fun-filled black-tie wedding celebration for 450 guests— on New Year's Eve. The grounds of her family's horse ranch offered plenty of space to erect several large tents for the reception. Because she wanted to hold the ceremony in her family home, we decided to limit the ceremony to eighty guests, and invite an additional 370 to the party.

As I probed Tamara about her tastes, preferences, and favorite things, I learned that she preferred simple foods but wanted an elegant menu for her party. She and her fiancé liked musicals, and were particularly fond of the works of Andrew Lloyd Webber. It was difficult to pin down her taste in decor, however, until I asked about her favorite films. Immediately, she brightened and told me how she had been captivated by the film *The Age of Innocence*. She loved the movie's elaborate, formal late-nineteenth-century decor and the rich look and baroque style of the antique furnishings. She particularly liked how the camera followed the characters through a succession of ornate rooms that were a true feast for the eyes. After our meeting was over, I saw the movie again and began to plan how we could re-create the unforgettable ambience and imagery of the film at Tamara's wedding.

On any other day, the living room of the bride's family home would look out onto green lawns with a corral and horse stables beyond. But this evening the view was of a series of massive white tents. The trees along the driveway, bare of leaves, were wrapped with large white bows and bathed in the glow of spotlights. Two enormous wreaths of pine, eucalyptus, Douglas fir, holly, and bright red roses decorated the front gateposts.

Inside the house, urns and vases of beautiful flowers were everywhere. The living room fireplace served as a backdrop for the ceremony and was adorned with thousands of ivory, pink, peach, and white roses, long-stemmed French tulips, English and variegated ivy, lightly gilded lemon leaves, and clusters of candles. A pair of tall standing candelabra, festooned with roses and trailing tendrils of ivy, bracketed the living room entrance.

Eighty close friends and family members took their seats as a piano and string quartet played classical compositions and popular music. Wearing long, form-fitting, midnight blue velvet gowns, the bridesmaids entered to the strains of Pachelbel's Canon in D Minor. To the music of "Saint Elmo's Fire," the tuxedo-clad groomsmen and groom Eric Gustavson, attired in a cream-colored shawl-collar dinner jacket, made their entrance. Then, as the quartet played "Music of the Night" from *Phantom of the Opera,* Tamara entered in a simple, off-the-shoulder, full-skirted silk-taffeta gown, carrying a cascade of soft pink, white, cream, and champagne-colored roses. A ceremony performed by the family minister united the couple, who chose "A Whole New World" from Disney's *Aladdin* for their recessional.

After the ceremony, the newlyweds joined their guests in the courtyard outside the house to await the other guests and enjoy champagne and appetizers while a harp and horns played classical music.

As the party guests arrived, they entered a foyer tent that opened into an eighty-foot carpeted hallway, with the receiving line stationed along one side. The opposite wall was lined with arched windows that provided views of the illuminated trees, with the Hughes home on the knoll beyond. At the entrance to the long hall, the guest book was set out

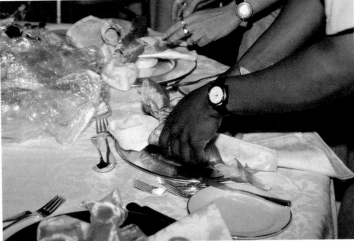

on an antique Louis XIV desk. At the hall's end stood an elaborately carved Regency console adorned with pink roses, under a gilded Venetian glass mirror. The furnishings were rented for the occasion from an antique shop. The lavish, opulent atmosphere, and the succession of rooms in which guests mingled during the cocktail party and through which they moved until they reached the ballroom tent, gave the evening a sense of anticipation and high drama. It also heightened the visual impact of the tented ballroom, elaborately decorated for this sumptuous celebration.

After moving through the receiving line, guests stepped into a six-thousand-square-foot, ornately draped dining marquis. Boldly colored floral arrangements in shades of deep red, fuchsia, purple, and gold made a dramatic statement against the backdrop of champagne carpeting and ivory walls. Rose-studded topiary centerpieces alternated with tall candelabra adorned with arrangements of vividly colored blooms and baby ivy. Heavy ivory damask cloths dressed the dinner tables, and the napkins were tied with gold mesh wired ribbon.

An arbor of ten-foot-tall Grecian columns draped with white tulle and cascades of roses, ranging in shades from the darkest red to the softest pink, showcased the bridal table. Down the center along the entire length of the table was an embankment of pink roses, flanked by two Victorian-style pomanders of pink roses at each end.

Guests were greeted by white-jacketed waiters holding trays of champagne, sparkling water, and hors d'oeuvres, with the band in full swing, playing Tamara and Eric's favorite big-band tunes. Later, dance music gave way to soft background music during a four-course dinner, which began with a mille-feuille (a flaky layered pastry) filled with chèvre, wild mushrooms, and tomato. A salad course—field greens with a slice of eggplant terrine and a crisp Parmesan crouton—followed. After a spirited round of dancing, guests were offered a choice of main course: stuffed chicken breast or roasted veal loin. Dessert was a rich warm apple tart with caramel sauce and vanilla ice cream.

Top right: Moments before the ceremony commenced, we double-checked to make sure that the rings would come off the pillow easily.

After dinner, the groom had a surprise. Eric took to the stage, not to make a toast or a speech, as many guests expected, but to sing "When a Man Loves a Woman" to his bride. His rendition brought tears to many eyes, including Tamara's.

The entire evening had been carefully orchestrated to culminate in the cake cutting at eleven-thirty and the New Year's Eve celebration at midnight. At the appointed hour, the bandleader called for the guests' attention; Tamara and Eric walked to the resplendent cake table, and together cut the first slice from their elaborate seven-tiered wedding cake, beautifully ornamented with gold leaf and translucent gold ribbon. The rest of the guests were served and toasted the happy couple with flutes of champagne.

Excitement began to build several minutes before midnight, as waiters passed festive party hats, horns, and noisemakers to the guests. At one minute before midnight, the lights in the tent began to dim and the countdown began. The lights went dark. As the clock tolled midnight, guests shouted "Happy New Year!" and the entire tent was illuminated with purple light. In a joyous burst of music, the band struck up "When the Saints Come Marching In"; the ceiling opened, and out poured thousands of white, gold, and silver balloons and 450 pounds of colored confetti on the delighted guests. Lights projected "Happy New Year"and "Tamara and Eric" onto the ceiling, and guests blew on their noisemakers and exchanged kisses and hugs.

At two A.M. the guests bade farewell. As guests departed, they received a copy of the *New York Times*, dated January 1, tied with white ribbon imprinted "Happy New Year from Tamara and Eric," and a bag of fresh bagels with cream cheese—a thoughtful gift to begin a wonderful new year.

APPETIZERS
Baby Potatoes Filled with Crème Fraîche and Osetra Caviar
Peking Duck Pancakes with Plum Sauce
Spring Lamb Chops with a Mint Pesto
Grilled Mediterranean Shrimp
Champagne Veuve Clicquot Brut in Magnums
Sparkling water

DINNER
Mille-Feuille of Phyllo Pastry with Chèvre, Wild Mushrooms, and Tomato
Salad of Baby Field Greens with Eggplant Terrine Dressed in a Sherry Vinegar and Olive Oil
Vinaigrette with a Parmesan Crouton
Groth Chardonnay 1991

Stuffed Breast of Chicken Served with a Bordelaise Sauce
Medley of Green Vegetables
Carrot Flan and Potatoes
Roasted Veal Loin with a Burgundy Sauce
Caymus Cabernet 1990 "Special Selection"

DESSERT
Apple Tart with Homemade Vanilla Ice Cream Served with a Burnt Caramel Sauce
Lemon Wedding Cake with White Chocolate Frosting and Fresh Berry Filling
Champagne Moet & Chandon Demi-Sec
Coffee

Although I knew Don Henley's music, I knew little of his personality. When I met Don to discuss his wedding, I quickly learned that this was a man who understood and appreciated quality. Don is a connoisseur of the first order, as exacting about the quality of his food, wine, and spirits as he is about the sound mix on an album. He made it clear from the very beginning that the celebration of his wedding to model Sharon Summerall was to feature the best of everything. Virtually every aspect of this celebration, from the card stock of the invitation to the vintage of the champagne, was exhaustively researched in order to provide the bride and groom with options that represented the ultimate in quality. No detail was too small to escape scrutiny.

Three days of festivities were planned on a spring weekend, beginning with a rehearsal dinner, followed by the wedding and a formal dinner for five hundred guests, and a brunch the following day. While Don and Sharon wanted their wedding reception to be elegant, in the sense that guests would wear formal dress, they insisted it be unpretentious and fun. Other festivities—the rehearsal dinner and the brunch—would be casual.

All events were to take place in the natural beauty of the outdoors, at the groom's home in a coastal canyon and at a nearby ranch, with tents, shade trees, and garden trellises providing shelter and comfort for guests. Don appreciated outdoor settings and particularly loved the look of the Irish countryside, with its lush vegetation and deep green grass. He and Sharon preferred the unruly appearance of flowers growing naturally in the wild to formal flower arrangements.

Topflight entertainment at the wedding was a major focus for this groom who played a significant role in creating some of the most popular songs in the history of rock music. Don also let me know that several musician friends would play at his wedding.

The fortunate friends and family invited to share in this springtime celebration knew they were in for something special from the moment the invitation, which was delivered by hand, arrived. The oversized envelope was composed of thick handmade ivory paper heavily embossed with a random pattern of leaves and fastened shut with a tiny bottle green satin bow. Inside was a three-paneled invitation engraved in celery green script, accented with gold edging, and lined with sheets of handmade, hand-torn tissue. A love poem by Elizabeth Barrett Browning appeared on one side panel; on the other, a personal note from Sharon and Don asked for guests' cooperation in keeping the events confidential and provided the name of a contact person to coordinate travel arrangements and handle guests' needs. The invitation was truly a piece of art in itself, and set the stage for the level of event that guests would experience.

When out-of-town guests arrived, they entered their hotel rooms to find an exquisitely crafted gift box constructed of the same ivory embossed card stock of the invitation and tied with a big bow of bottle green, wired-satin ribbon. Inside, nestled in fragrant pine shavings, were a bottle of mineral water, two perfectly ripe pears, a scented candle, and an array of organic skin and bath products selected by the bride and groom. A note from Sharon and Don thanked each guest for traveling to share in the celebration and outlined the weekend's events, including pickup times and locations.

The weekend began with some down-home fun—an authentic Southwestern barbecue. For an evening, the grounds of Don's canyon

ranch were transformed into a little corner of Texas, the home state of both the bride and groom. Next to Don's barn, redwood benches and tables covered in red checkered cloths were set under a spacious garden canopy. Riotous arrangements of sunflowers and wildflowers were displayed in rough-hewn wooden crates on the tables, and a gleaming vintage jukebox was loaded with the groom's favorite tunes.

For the food, a bit of Texas was imported. Al Callaway, who owns Squares barbecue restaurant in Abilene, drove halfway across the country towing his huge smoker to cater the dinner. As guests arrived at Don's home and entered the backyard, they were greeted by plumes of fragrant smoke rising from the barbecue and the sounds of rock-and-roll tunes from the jukebox. Family and friends mingled, sampling appetizers and sipping on IBC root beer, Coca-Cola in old-fashioned six-ounce glass bottles, Big Red (a Texas soft drink), and an array of icy beers. Soon Sharon, Don, and the rest of the wedding party, who had been rehearsing the nuptials at the wedding site nearby, arrived and the festivities began. The great food, lively music, and informal atmosphere made for a rollicking good time.

At the wedding site, a beautiful ranch in the hills, preparations had begun two weeks earlier with the planting of hundreds of wildflowers and irrigation of the meadows to create a lush vista for the wedding day. To shelter guests seated for the ceremony, an airy enclosure was built of dark green latticework and covered with luxuriant vines and full-blown pale pink, ivory, pale yellow, and champagne-colored roses. Candelabra were hung from the rafters and festooned with moss, ivy, vines, and more roses. The effect was of a vast arbor that, over time, had become thickly overgrown with wild vines and flowers. Surrounding the ceremony site, more than a thousand tall pillar candles were placed directly on the grass.

For the post-ceremony cocktail reception, a tennis court was enclosed by framework draped with hundreds of yards of snowy white chiffon. Bottle green carpeting covered the court surface. Boxwood topiaries covered with unruly arrangements of vines and roses decorated the interior.

Nearby, a twelve-thousand-square-foot semipermanent tented structure was erected to provide space for dining and dancing for the five hundred guests. The ballroom was reached through an entry hall leading into a spacious tented rotunda, which was hung with paintings and lined with antique furniture. In the center of the rotunda stood an antique Biedermeier table holding an enormous floral arrangement. From the rotunda, an entryway led into the main ballroom, which had been designed to look like a permanent structure with inset windows swagged with curtains and tiebacks made from clusters of orange Sensation roses. In the center of the room next to the stage was a sunken dance floor. The area for dancing was bordered with garden boxes filled with privet hedging that was covered with honeysuckle vines and mosses and studded with roses.

The ballroom's large stage, lined on each side with heavy ivory draping and four-tiered stone fountains overflowing with roses, provided plenty of room to showcase the evening's entertainment. For two days before the big event, the stage was one of the busiest areas on the ranch as the entertainers loaded in their equipment and conducted sound checks. The other hub of activity was the kitchen, where renowned chef Emeril

Top left: During the ceremony, a heavy fog rolled in off the Pacific. The candles shining through the mist gave an unworldly atmosphere to the evening.

Floral tiebacks which were created from pavéed roses attached to florist's oasis in a chicken-wire frame. Actual windows were inserted in the walls of the dining marquee to create an indoor-outdoor feeling. The tent was transformed into a stately interior with the use of antique furniture, artwork, mirrors, and flowers. The six-layer wedding cake, lavishly draped in thin sheets of white chocolate, was showcased in the center of the ballroom as guests entered.

Lagasse of Emeril's in New Orleans—one of Don's favorite restaurants—was putting the finishing touches on a menu of Louisiana-style specialties.

Hundreds of hours of preparation came together in the late afternoon of a sunny Saturday in May as guests began to arrive. While Sharon was ensconced with her mother and bridesmaids in a dressing room near the ceremony area, Don and his ushers made their final preparations in their dressing room. Guests mingled, sipping fresh lemonade under the shade of a spreading oak tree, while a harpist played classical melodies. As the sun began to set, the pillar candles placed around the ceremony area bathed the meadow in a soft light.

A classical quartet near the entrance to the seating area began to play, signaling the start of the nuptials. Under the trellised arbor, an orchestra composed of members of the Los Angeles Chamber Orchestra played a Bach concerto as guests took their seats. Then, to the lilting melody of Handel's *Water Music*, the procession began with the entrance of the minister, the groom and his best man, the families of the bride and groom, the bridesmaids, and the groomsmen.

As the orchestra played the first bars of Beethoven's Romance No. 2 in F, the bride entered on the arm of her father, wearing an off-the-shoulder Christian Dior gown. The ceremony was officiated by the minister from Sharon's church in Dallas. Toward the end of the ceremony, almost like magic, a bank of fog rolled in, creating an ethereal effect as the candles outside shimmered through the mist. When the groom had kissed his bride, the wedding party filed out to the joyous strains of Mozart's Symphony No. 37 in G Major.

While photos were being taken of the bridal party, guests were escorted down a meandering garden path to the cocktail reception. Here, the musical mood changed to upbeat Irish melodies by the Chieftains, along with two Irish folk dancers, who had flown in specifically to perform at Sharon and Don's wedding. Guests were treated to a forty-five-minute set of the Chieftains' hits as waiters passed glasses of Champagne Krug Clos de Mesnil 1976 and an array of spicy hors d'oeuvres prepared by Chef Lagasse. Four caviar bars showcased mounds of Russian beluga caviar on ice, with appropriate accompaniments. Shots from bottles of Stolichnaya, Ketel One, and Absolut vodka, which had been frozen in decorative ice molds, were offered with the caviar.

When dinner was announced, waiters escorted guests into the dining marquee, where the Frank Capp Orchestra was performing big-band tunes from the 1940s. As guests entered the ballroom, they immediately saw the towering six-layer wedding cake, which stood four feet high off the cake table. Each layer was draped in a thin sheet of white chocolate that looked like the finest silk, gathered at the top of each layer with pale yellow Message roses. Beyond the cake, the room was a sea of beautiful ivory fabrics—damask covered the tables, gabardine covered the chairs, and the tent walls were entirely lined with pleated silk. On the center of each table was a tightly packed arrangement of roses in varying shades of ivory, white, pale yellow, and gold wrapped in tendrils of blooming honeysuckle for an overgrown look. Over the dance floor hung a huge chandelier entirely blanketed with thousands of roses.

To get the party off to a romantic start, Don and Sharon headed straight to the dance floor for their first dance as a married couple to Glenn Miller's "Moonlight Serenade." After several minutes, the bride and groom's respective families joined the bridal couple on the dance floor. As the dance tunes ended, the bandleader took the music down in volume, signaling the start of dinner.

The four-course menu, developed by Chef Lagasse, featured an appetizer of barbecued shrimp with rosemary biscuits, followed by an Acadian-style country gumbo, served tableside. The main course, free-range chicken marinated in Creole spices and grilled over hickory wood, was presented with traditional Louisiana-style accompaniments, including crawfish spoon bread, greens, and pecan gravy. After a spirited round of dancing, dessert—apple pie with a cheddar cheese crust and spiced cream—was served.

At the close of another dance set, the master of ceremonies—a close friend of the groom's—signaled for attention and Sharon and Don stepped to the center of the room to cut the wedding cake, which was made to Don's specifications from his mother's recipe. Special Texas pecans for the cake had been air-freighted to the baker via overnight courier. Sharon and Don fed each other the traditional first bites of cake and the waiters served cake and champagne to guests.

The evening's entertainment began with a special appearance by an artist for whom Don holds the greatest respect: Tony Bennett. Accompanied by a trio of world-class musicians, Tony treated the audience to a twenty-minute set of his favorite ballads. As guests listened, they also had an opportunity to sample fine imported cigars and select after-dinner drinks from carts that were rolled from table to table.

It was nearly midnight by the time Tony Bennett sang his last encore, but the night was young and there was anticipation in the air as the change-over of instruments was taking place behind the stage curtain. Next up: Sting, the first in a series of Don's friends, including Bruce Springsteen, Billy Joel, Sheryl Crow, Jackson Browne, J. D. Souther, and John Fogerty, who each performed songs they chose together with the bride and groom. Finally, Don himself took to the stage to the cheers of the excited audience. A look around the tables at guests' enraptured faces made it clear everyone knew they were witnessing a once-in-a-lifetime concert.

In the early hours of the morning, rock group Jack Mack and the Heart Attack took over for an energetic set as guests enjoyed a buffet breakfast of scrambled eggs, sausages, and smoked salmon. When the set was over, the bride and groom made their exit to the honeymoon suite of a nearby beach hotel, and guests reluctantly headed home. Guests returning to their hotel rooms found a tiny box of Teuscher champagne chocolate truffles and a personal note from Sharon and Don on their pillows—a sweet end to an incomparable evening.

A casual, outdoor brunch at Don's ranch the following day was prudently scheduled to begin no earlier than noon, allowing everyone to sleep in. The spacious canopy that had sheltered a Southwestern barbecue was transformed into a spring showcase, draped with yards of sunny yellow chiffon. Round tables covered with cheerful yellow and white cloths, and centerpieces of masses of yellow daffodils planted in wooden crates, replaced the picnic tables. Guests toasted the bride and groom with champagne bellinis (champagne with fresh peach juice) and feasted on a lavish brunch buffet that included made-to-order omelettes, grilled sausages, rolled salmon stuffed with spinach, and a variety of side dishes.

The relaxing setting allowed guests to reflect on the wedding that seemed like a fantasy—but turned out to be an experience no one would ever forget.

Bottom left: Chef Emeril Lagasse proudly presents his appetizers for the cocktail reception.

WEDDING RECEPTION DINNER CREATED BY EMERIL LAGASSE

APPETIZERS
Spicy Crawfish Boulettes with Creole Mustard and Honey Dipping Sauce
Goat Cheese in Herbed Phyllo Wraps
Smothered Barbecue Beef Salad in Chili Profiteroles
Louisiana Blue Crab Cakes with Jalapeño Tartar Sauce
Smoked Mushroom Strudel with Spicy Dipping Sauce
Lobster Cheesecake Bites on Endive with a Green Onion Coulis
Caviar Buffet with Accoutrements
Champagne Krug Clos de Mesnil 1976
Sparkling water
Frozen vodkas in ice molds

DINNER
Emeril's New Orleans Barbecued Shrimp with
Little Homemade Rosemary Biscuits
An Acadian-Style Country Gumbo Served with Steamed Louisiana Rice

Organically Grown Free-Range Chicken Marinated with Creole Spices,
Hickory Grilled, and Served with Corn Bread, Crawfish Spoon Bread,
Southern Cooked Greens, Sweet Potatoes, and Pecan Gravy

Byron Chardonnay Reserve 1993
Ceretto Barolo Zonchera 1990

DESSERT
Apple Pie with Cheddar Cheese Crust and Spiced Cream
Texas Pecan Wedding Cake with Whipped Cream Frosting
and White Chocolate Draping
Champagne Krug 1985

N ow that you have seen how other brides and grooms created their weddings, it is time for you to think about your own celebration. Leave your assumptions at the door and start from scratch. Ask yourself the questions that I ask each bride and groom. Be sure to involve your fiancé, too. Your responses to these questions will enable you to begin developing a concept that will guide your wedding plans.

When you have answered the questions, make notes about your responses and what they indicate about your personal style. Think carefully about which questions and answers seem most important to you. These may be the issues that will be most crucial to the design of your celebration.

Based on your answers, begin to put together the big picture of your celebration. Your answers will indicate whether your wedding should be held in a certain season or at a certain time of day. You'll quickly see whether an indoor or an outdoor wedding is most appropriate. The style of your celebration will emerge—a formal or informal event, a lunch or a dinner.

As part of the wedding planning process, you may also wish to carry around a small notebook or cassette recorder, or enter your thoughts on your personal computer. Note wedding-related things you like—and dislike. Both are equally important. Keep track of wedding-related ideas that come to you during the day or night.

In addition to looking inward for wedding ideas, use all the resources at your disposal. Bridal magazines are an excellent source of ideas. But other magazines, such as those that cover fashion, food, and home and garden subjects, are filled with wonderful ideas on attire, decor, and sharing celebrations with friends. Even mail-order catalogs can be a source of intriguing styles and products that might tie into your wedding celebration. Clip articles and photos that strike you as attractive or interesting, and keep them in a folder to help during the planning process and to show to vendors, such as your wedding planner, florist, rental company, or dressmaker.

COLIN'S QUESTIONS FOR BRIDES AND GROOMS

1. **What are your favorite restaurants?** Describe why you like them—the atmosphere, type of cuisine, quality of food, the way the food is served, and perhaps the way the restaurant is decorated. If there is an element that your favorite restaurants have in common, what is it? What is it about your favorite restaurants that you might wish to incorporate into a great wedding reception?

2. **What are your favorite foods?** Are there types of foods—French, northern Italian, Indian, Japanese, Southwestern barbecue—that you love? What are your least favorite foods? Are there certain dishes from favorite restaurants that you love, such as a grilled vegetable salad, or the way a local bistro prepares duck breast? This information will help you better direct your caterer.

3. **What sort of food service do you prefer?** Is a formal sit-down dinner your idea of an ideal party? Or do you prefer a buffet, where you can pick and choose? Do you enjoy dining casually or more formally?

4. **What are your favorite drinks?** Do you prefer wine, beer, spirits, or soft drinks? Do you have a favorite cocktail? Does your fiancé love microbrews?

5. Where do you like to spend your vacation? What appeals to you about this destination, and why? Is it formal or relaxed? Cosmopolitan or rustic? On the beach or in the country?

6. What are your favorite books or stories? What sort of atmosphere does your favorite book or story create? Are there ways to incorporate elements of this into a wedding celebration?

7. What is your favorite film, and why do you like it? Are there scenes from a favorite movie that really speak to you? Do you remember wedding scenes that you love from films, such as the nuptials in *Four Weddings and a Funeral* or *Father of the Bride?*

8. What is your favorite flower? Are there flowers you dislike? If you don't know the specific names of flowers, think about what colors and types of flowers appeal to you. Look through books and magazines, and note or clip photos of the ones you like.

9. What are your favorite and least favorite colors? Consider how your favorite colors translate to different types of fabrics that might be used in wedding attire or decor. You may even find samples in your wardrobe or sewing box.

10. Does a particular time of day or season of the year inspire you? Do you love sunsets? Do you love the cozy feeling of being indoors after a winter snowfall? Do you love long summer evenings outdoors? How might you translate this to your wedding?

11. Do you have a favorite collection that might offer a theme for your wedding? Perhaps you collect majolica, vintage linens, or crystal decanters. Incorporating a collection of beautiful things that have meaning to the bride or groom is a lovely way to personalize a wedding celebration.

12. Do you have a hobby or pursuit that you want to incorporate into your wedding in some way? If a couple loves to sail, a seaside wedding at a marina, yacht club, or even on a boat might be appropriate. If you love opera, perhaps your celebration should include some of your favorite arias performed by a local opera singer. If you enjoy collecting wine, then fine wine might be a focus of your celebration.

13. What clothing designers are your favorites? What specifically about their designs appeals to you? Is it the lines of the clothing, the use of color, the fabrics? Is there a fabric you are particularly fond of, a trim you have always admired, a silhouette you love?

14. Do you have a fairy-tale image of being a bride from your childhood? Do you have a childhood wedding fantasy? Or a contemporary one?

15. Do you see your wedding as a single event, or would you like to have a series of events over several days, such as a weekend-long celebration?

16. What is your favorite type of music? Make a list of your favorite composers and their works, or artists and their songs. Be sure to make a short list of the music you definitely do *not* want to hear at your wedding!

17. What are your favorite photographic styles? Do you like black and white, color, or sepia? Do you like a photojournalistic, documentary, or traditional portrait approach?

18. When you can do absolutely anything, or nothing at all, how do you spend the day? Would you love to spend a day pampering yourself at a salon, or would you prefer a great hike in the mountains? How could you translate that to your wedding day? What special magic is there in that choice?

Left: Comfortable furniture, elegant residential lighting, and dreamy gauze draping creates a soft and romantic effect.

THE BUDGET

Of course, you can't plan a wedding in a vacuum. While taking inspiration from your personal taste and style, you will, of course, need to be realistic. There are three major factors that will help you determine your direction as you design your wedding: budget, guest list, and venue.

Budget is the first factor. Once you have the overall approach to your wedding in mind, your budget will define the choices you make and the parameters of what you can and can't do.

Today, it is no longer an assumption that the bride's parents pay for the wedding. While it is still common for the bride's family to pay for the majority of the wedding expenses, it is also common for the groom's family to contribute. Quite often the bride and groom pay for their own wedding. However you expect to pay for your nuptial celebration, you can't begin to design a wedding until you have a budget.

Remember that style is not related to how much money you have to spend. Regardless of budget, everyone can create an elegant wedding that guests will enjoy. A wedding doesn't have to be expensive to be memorable. Guests don't necessarily expect a formal sit-down dinner and dancing until dawn. Your friends might well prefer to have fun at a chic cocktail party, attend an elegant afternoon tea, or partake in a festive champagne breakfast.

At its most basic, a wedding is the ceremony that unites the two of you. Everything else is up for grabs. There's no rule that says you have to wear white, serve expensive French champagne, sit for formal portrait photographs, have a dinner, or serve a layered wedding cake. I always tell brides who are agonizing about the decisions they have to make in planning their weddings that guests will never know the choices they made. When you serve delicious mimosas (sparkling wine and orange juice) at your reception, guests will be delighted. They will never know you did it to save money on sparkling wine.

I always encourage new ideas and alternative approaches to wedding celebrations. Instead of a gala evening incorporating ten elements, pick three or four and do them well. A cocktail party for sixty guests with good champagne, tasty hors d'oeuvres, and a great jazz trio is a fabulous approach to a wedding reception, and it just happens to be less expensive than a sit-down dinner. Taking an alternative approach to the flower arrangements, like using gypsophila as the single flower in all the centerpieces, is a marvelous idea that has tremendous visual impact and, incidentally, is less expensive than traditional floral arrangements.

Instead of expensive French champagne, why not give guests a choice of flavored martinis from a martini bar, with nonalcoholic drinks in stemmed martini glasses for the nondrinkers? I guarantee your guests will be absolutely delighted and will never miss the bubbly. If you don't need dozens of formal wedding photos, skip the formal shots and hire a photographer who understands the photojournalistic approach to snap lots of candids at the reception. The bridal party can then go directly from the ceremony to the party to celebrate with the guests, and everyone will have more fun. Plus, you won't spend as much money.

Keep in mind that with weddings, the highest-cost items are generally food and beverages and equipment rentals, such as tents, tables, and chairs. Thus, these are the areas where efforts to contain costs will have the most impact. Instead of skimping on the standard approach, make

The choice of a wine to serve at a wedding reception can range from an inexpensive, high-quality bottling from California to the best of Bordeaux.

different, creative choices and you'll have a great celebration that fits your personality and your budget.

No matter how much money you have budgeted for your wedding, you are spending hard-earned dollars. You want to make sure that you spend your money thoughtfully and with care, to create a celebration that makes a personal statement from you and your groom, and gives your guests an occasion to remember.

THE GUEST LIST

Because so many other wedding-related decisions depend upon the number of guests, it is important to create your guest list early on. The number of guests will affect the cost of your wedding and where you want to hold your ceremony and reception.

In developing your list, think about what your wedding means to you. People are invited to a wedding in order to share in the happiness of the bridal couple and celebrate their union. The idea is to surround yourself with the nearest and dearest people to you and your groom. You need not feel obliged to invite all your parents' friends, distant relatives, your coworkers, and your friends' children to your wedding. Weddings are no place for mere acquaintances or strangers. Traditionally, the guest list is divided equally between the bride and groom, but even here there is room for flexibility depending on the actual number of people each side of the family wishes to invite.

As you work on your guest list, think about the kinds of people who will attend. Is it a lively bunch that loves to dance, or is it a sophisticated set that enjoys spirited conversation and great food? Is it a dressy group or a casual crowd? You want to create a gathering where you and your guests will be comfortable and have a great time.

Once you have a guest list and budget, determine within your budget what is the absolute best party you can have. Again, this is not a matter of figuring out the most expensive party but the type of celebration that fits you, your groom, and your guests.

In some cases, you may wish to rethink your guest list if your concept is too costly for the number of people you would like to invite. On the other hand, if you and your fiancé have a large circle of good friends and dozens of close relatives with whom you want to celebrate, consider an alternative approach to the traditional sit-down dinner, such as a clambake on the beach, a Sunday morning brunch, or an outdoor luncheon on a country farm. If your guest list is truly vast and your budget is not, time your wedding to occur between meals and offer a limited menu, which can be as simple as a delicious sparkling wine punch and wedding cake. It may be preferable to share a joyous occasion simply, with the many people who are close to you, rather than hold a lavish reception for just a few.

LOCATION

Another decision that relates to designing your wedding is your choice of venue, the place or places where you will hold your ceremony and reception. Wedding locations generally fall into two categories. There are self-contained locations, such as hotels, country clubs, and catering halls, which provide all the amenities and services needed for a typical wedding—food and beverages, tables and chairs, linens, china and serving pieces, and waiters. This type of location may be easier and more convenient for brides, because all the services are coordinated centrally. On the other hand, you may lack the freedom to utilize the vendors *you* want.

The alternative is an off-site location, which offers few or no services on the premises. These include private homes, and rental spaces such as ranches, wineries, historic houses, or museums.

The style of your wedding will tend to dictate the type of venue that is appropriate, whether it is a farm with a charming old barn, a chic night-club, or an elegant hotel ballroom. In some cases your venue may already be predetermined—for example, if you have long wanted an at-home wedding, or if you have a favorite minister at your church. Then you need to create your vision within the parameters of the space you have.

When looking for wedding venues, keep in mind that it is always easiest to hold the ceremony and reception at the same site. This approach also allows you to save money by moving flowers and decor elements from the ceremony to the reception. However, it is perfectly workable to have your ceremony and reception at two different sites, as long as they are within twenty minutes' driving time of each other. If your ceremony and reception sites are far apart, consider providing transportation, such as vans or buses, for the guests.

As you narrow your choices for a venue, be sure that you ask about any and all rules in effect at the site. Some venues have stringent regulations about what can and cannot be done there in terms of food service, decor, music, or parking. You don't want to find this out when it is too late to change locations.

Consider also whether you want to hold additional events planned around your celebration, and how these will work with the venue you have chosen. I am noticing that more and more couples build their wedding into a weekend-long celebration, beginning with a rehearsal dinner and culminating with a post-wedding brunch and send-off for the honeymooning couple. This approach works particularly well if many guests will be traveling to your wedding from out of town.

SETTING THE DATE

Some brides and grooms set a date for their wedding and it works perfectly for all parties. Often, however, the initial date must be changed for a variety of reasons. Sometimes the date has to be changed after booking several wedding vendors.

If you are changing your wedding date, be sure to alert everyone who was told of the previous date. I have seen it happen many times that a bride has changed dates and was sure she had notified all her vendors—but forgot to tell the baker. She and the baker continue to have productive conversations about the wedding cake; the bride fails to notice the different date on the contract, and guess what? The cake arrives a week early! Avoid this by confirming the new date with all your vendors.

REGISTERING FOR GIFTS

In my line of business I have the opportunity to talk to groups of brides on a regular basis. I often ask the brides to indicate by a show of hands how many of them inherited china. You would be surprised to learn how many of them raise their hands. Further questioning generally reveals that they seldom, if ever, use the china, and neither did their parents!

Too many of us pride ourselves in creating beautiful homes that we are too busy to enjoy, and collecting wonderful things that we don't use. As you plan your new life with your husband-to-be, remember that there is no better way to invest quality time with one another than to invite friends and family into your home. Your bridal registry is a wonderful opportunity to select items that you will use and that will bring your home to life.

When creating your bridal registry, choose items that reflect your lifestyle. If you live casually and entertain informally, don't register for an elaborate, formal china pattern that you will be afraid to use and that will sit in the closet and collect dust. Consider a more creative approach, such as a mix-and-match set of china or dinnerware that can accommodate a variety of entertaining styles. Look for sets of dinner plates, salad and dessert plates, cups and saucers that are different in pattern but compatible in color and style. You can even mix the offerings of different manufacturers as long as the patterns work with each other. This approach allows you to reinvent your table settings by adding and changing elements. It is a much more interesting look that allows your personal style to show in your table settings.

Remember, too, that bridal registration is not limited to tabletop. Leading department stores and mass merchants make it easy to register for bedding, linens, furniture, and artwork. Many couples not only register for housewares, but for luggage, home electronics, musical recordings, and even camping equipment.

LOGISTICS

As your plans begin to take shape, consider who will assist you with the arrangements for your nuptials. There are several options, including wedding consultants, experienced caterers, a close friend, your maid or matron of honor, and your mother.

If you are hiring a professional to manage your wedding arrangements, it is very important to develop a rapport with this individual and be confident that he or she is sensitive and receptive to your ideasand preferences. If you choose not to hire a professional wedding planner, consider asking a well-organized friend to manage the details of your wedding, perhaps for an agreed-upon fee. While many brides are capable of designing and managing a fabulous wedding, take it from me: you don't want to be bothered with last-minute details on your wedding day.

No matter how resourceful and talented they may be, many brides become nervous and panicky about their upcoming wedding. Don't let this happen to you. Planning a wedding is not about working yourself to a frazzle for weeks in order to have fun on your wedding day. You should be having fun during the *entire process* of planning your wedding—selecting your flowers, choosing your dress, finalizing your invitations, hearing from old friends—straight through to your honeymoon. This is a joyous time. If you are not enjoying the design and planning process, you're missing out. Something's wrong. Identify what is causing your anxiety, and find a solution to the problem. Seize the opportunity to have fun and enjoy this unique moment in your life.

Planning a wedding is not the same thing as writing a term paper that gets an A, or successfully managing a major project at work. I have known a few brides who have been so obsessed with making everything perfect that they got hives two weeks before the wedding. The day came and went, and it wasn't a pleasurable experience for them. They were too intent on doing it flawlessly. It's not about that. You will not be judged on the perfection of your wedding. You get no medals.

But if you approach your wedding with creativity and a sense of fun, you'll enjoy it from start to finish and remember it the rest of your life. And so will your guests!

Left: Mismatched linens and several Lenox china patterns may be combined for an endless variety of table settings.

WEDDING GIFTS AND THANK-YOU NOTES

At wedding after wedding, I notice guests arriving at the ceremony or reception with gifts. When gifts are brought to a wedding, they must be secured during the party, and then transported. Often this creates logistical problems, particularly if the bride and groom are leaving on their honeymoon immediately after the reception. It is more considerate to send the gift before or after the wedding. The one exception is if the wedding is being held at home, where it is perfectly acceptable to bring gifts.

Remember that wedding gifts may be sent up to the couple's first anniversary. That doesn't mean that the bride has the same latitude with thank-you notes! Thank-you notes should be mailed within six weeks of receiving the gift. If you had a very large wedding and cannot complete all the thank-you notes promptly, preprinted cards may be sent indicating that the gift was received and a personal note will follow.

If you have a large wedding and receive many presents, I recommend using a Polaroide camera as you open them. Snap a picture of each gift and jot down the name of the giver and any other important notes on the back of each photo. Small gifts may be grouped several to a photo. This will make the process of writing thank-you notes much easier, particularly if it is a job that you tackle a couple of weeks after the wedding when you return from your honeymoon.

s the first piece of communication your guests receive, the invitation sets the tone for your celebration. The invitation is a window into your wedding. While family and friends may know the date of your nuptials well in advance, it is when they open your invitation that they begin to envision the style of your celebration. The basic "who, what, where, and when" information should be communicated with style—the style that will be woven throughout your wedding.

Creating a beautiful invitation requires research and creativity. In fact, because wedding invitations must often be ordered at least three months in advance, this should be one of your first undertakings after you have located your venue, determined your guest list, and conceptualized your celebration.

There used to be only one "correct" style of wedding invitation: engraved in black typeface on heavy white or ecru card stock, using traditional wording. But with today's relaxed social rules, families taking a wide range of configurations, and ceremonies running the gamut from informal to traditional, there is plenty of opportunity for flexibility and creativity. I encourage innovation in wedding invitations—using beautiful handmade paper, choosing an unusual ink color, or incorporating a gorgeous silk ribbon or tie. At the same time, I like to keep invitations simple and tasteful. A beautiful invitation that exudes your personal sense of style will fill your guests with a sense of anticipation and excitement, setting the stage for a wonderful celebration.

The important guiding principles are taste and appropriateness. The invitation should fit the affair you are planning.

When designing an invitation, think about the style and level of formality (or informality) of your ceremony and the celebration to follow. If you are planning a traditional church wedding with an evening reception at an elegant hotel, the design of your invitation should reflect this level of formality, perhaps by using engraved script on heavy ecru card stock with a beveled edge.

An at-home wedding with the reception in your garden might call for a less traditional approach, perhaps using pale green colors, or a garden motif or icon in the printed materials.

Is there a theme or motif for your wedding? Vanessa Angel's last name provided a motif that was woven throughout her wedding, and first appeared on the invitations, which were embossed with a pair of tiny gold cherubs.

While you are thinking about design, consider how much information the invitation must convey. A simple ceremony and reception at the same site requires only an invitation, reply card, and return envelope. If the reception is held at a different site from the ceremony, there may be a separate reception insert. When other events are being held around the wedding, such as a rehearsal dinner or post-wedding brunch, invitations to those gatherings may be included as well. If necessary, maps or driving instructions to the ceremony and reception may also be included. Some couples want to convey a personal message to guests, or perhaps incorporate a favorite quote or poem.

Many couples turn their wedding into the central event of festivities that last for several days or a weekend. In such a case, the invitation should be designed as a unified, complete package that provides all the information about your celebration that a guest might need. When you

plan carefully in advance, your invitation can work as a coherent whole, not as an unwieldy package of cards, envelopes, and maps. For example, a creative invitation designer might fashion a three-paneled folder designed to hold several invitations, reply cards, maps, and other elements, by fastening the pieces to each panel with ribbon that is either glued on or threaded through holes in the card stock. This approach conveys a great deal of information in a simple and elegant package, while allowing the bride to customize the invitations by including only the appropriate items for each guest.

An important first step is to identify your invitation supplier. Many brides obtain their invitations through a stationery store. A good stationer should have a wedding specialist on staff who is conversant with wedding etiquette and both traditional and nontraditional wording. The wedding specialist should be able to show you books containing the range of options in ink colors and paper stocks, and provide samples of different printing processes.

A custom-designed invitation is another option for a couple seeking a unique look. A custom design lets you create an invitation that is one of a kind. Today's designers often work with distinctive and unusual materials, such as handmade or textured papers, floral and plant materials, fabrics, paints, or gilding. Keep in mind that custom-designed invitations often require even more lead time than engraved invitations to develop and refine the design or artwork.

No matter whom you choose to work with, I can't stress enough how critical it is to carefully check wording, addresses, and all the components you will need to avoid costly or embarrassing errors. Always obtain a copy of all materials before they are printed, and have several people proof them in addition to yourself.

It is very important to determine early on how many guests will be invited and to order a sufficient quantity of invitations. Typically, you will need one invitation per household, although children older than sixteen and single adults who are roommates should each receive a separate invitation. Be generous in your estimate; the cost of printing a few extra invitations is nothing compared to the cost of having to go to a second printing if you fail to order a sufficient quantity. Also, order at least twenty-five extra envelopes (both outer and inner, if your invitation includes one) to allow for mistakes in hand-addressing.

MATERIALS

There are two kinds of paper stock: those based on wood pulp, and those based on cotton fibers or "rag" papers. The most formal invitations use cotton rag paper because it has a richer, more refined look and feel, and it will not yellow or decompose over time. Traditional wedding invitations have a fold on the left side. They may be ordered plain, or with a panel that is blind embossed to frame the text.

INK COLORS AND STYLE

The most formal invitations are engraved in black ink. But many beautiful invitations feature ink in offbeat colors, such as celery green, hunter green, chocolate brown, tea, or cranberry. Select a type style that suits the level of formality and style of your wedding.

UPDATING THE CLASSIC INVITATION

When a couple wants a traditional look to their invitation but feels that classic black printing is too somber, I often suggest using a colored ink that picks up on a hue we intend to use in their wedding. An invitation in hunter green or glossy chocolate brown script, printed on heavy ecru stock, offers a fresh twist while keeping all the elegance of the traditional approach. For a wedding during the holiday season, consider using cranberry-colored ink and lining the envelope with a rich paisley-printed paper. Another idea is to use a border around the invitation that picks up a design motif of your wedding—ivy, flowers, grapevines, seashells, architectural elements—whatever fits your style.

WORKING WITH A CALLIGRAPHER

Calligraphy gives a beautiful finishing touch to envelopes, place cards, even the invitation itself if desired. Most stationery stores have their own calligrapher or can recommend an outside source. Talk with several calligraphers and look at samples to get a sense of their style. If your invitation is printed in script or in colored ink, the calligrapher should be able to replicate the style of the script and the color of ink on the envelopes.

It is also possible to have a skilled calligrapher hand-letter all the elements of your invitation, which are then printed. The same calligrapher can hand-letter your envelopes, place cards, host cards, and menus in the same style, giving your wedding a unified look.

MAILING

Whether your invitation is traditional or custom-made, make sure it conforms in size to U.S. Postal Service regulations and take care to affix the correct postage. Heavy paper stock and multiple pieces often require additional postage. If you are going to be mailing your own invitations, bring one entire invitation with all the inserts to your post office to have it weighed and measured. Obtain attractive stamps in the correct amount of postage at the same time.

PRINTING METHODS

Depending on the look you want to achieve with your invitation, there is a range of printing methods to consider.

•A traditional engraved invitation uses an expensive, age-old process of preparing a copper plate that is then imprinted on heavy paper. This produces raised printing and a slight impression on the reverse side of the card. Engraved invitations may be ordered through fine stationery stores and usually require four to six weeks for printing. Traditionally, engraved invitations were always accompanied by a tissue overlay to avoid smudging; while this is no longer necessary, the tradition lives on as an option.

•Thermography is a raised ink printing process that looks very similar to engraving but is much less costly. This is a popular way to achieve a classic engraved look on a budget.

•Letterpress is an old-fashioned printing process that yields a unique, handmade look.

•Conventional flat printing is another option, perhaps using a motif or icon that ties in to the style of your wedding.

WHEN TO SEND

Timing is an important issue. The invitation must be mailed far enough in advance so that your guests can easily plan to attend. If many guests are traveling from out of town to your wedding, a save-the-date card sent out several months in advance is thoughtful. The standard schedule for invitations is as follows:

Order invitations	2 to 3 months in advance
Mail save-the-date card	Up to 3 months in advance
Mail invitation	6 to 8 weeks in advance
Mail rehearsal dinner invitation (if separate)	3 to 4 weeks in advance
Mail post-wedding brunch invitation	With wedding invitation, if desired; otherwise 3 to 4 weeks in advance

INVITATION COMPONENTS

Be sure to think through all your invitation-related needs so that you can place one order and save time and money.

Save-the-date card—These are typically used when the wedding will be held out of town or when many guests are traveling to the wedding from afar. The save-the-date card is usually quite simple and is mailed up to three months before the wedding. If appropriate, it could include the name of a travel agent who is coordinating wedding travel, and/or the hotel name and contact information.

Invitation to ceremony (and reception, if held at the same site).

Reception card if the reception is to be held at a different site from the ceremony.

Invitation envelope(s)—With traditional formal invitations, there is an outer envelope, which is mailed, and an inner envelope that protects the invitation. The outer envelope is always addressed by hand. If there is an inner envelope, it too is hand-addressed with the recipient's title and last name only: "Mr. and Mrs. Smith," or "Dr. Jones." The tradition of the outer and inner envelope dates back to the days when invitations would be delivered by horsemen. The inner envelope protected the invitation from the perils of the journey.

Reply card and stamped, self-addressed envelope—The reply card

115

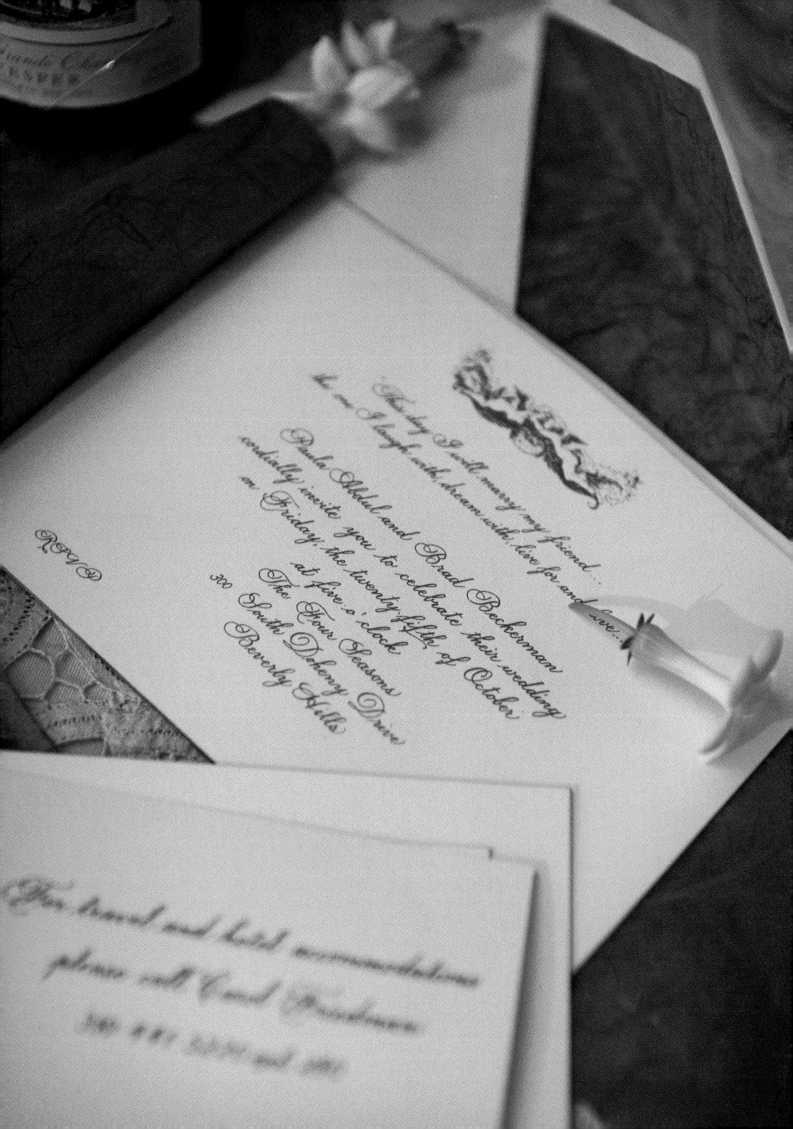

simply reads, "M _____ will/will not attend." If budget permits, you could have these personalized with each recipient's name hand-lettered by a calligrapher. The reply card often includes a "please reply by (date)" line. Note: before mailing, number the back of each reply card and code it to your guest list in case a guest replies but fails to add his or her name or the handwriting is illegible.

Historically, reply cards were not included with wedding invitations because guests were expected to hand-write a personal note of response that incorporated the wording of the invitation: "Mr. Charles P. Howland accepts with pleasure the kind invitation of Mr. and Mrs. Sidney Mellon to the wedding of their daughter . . ." While reply cards are optional, most people include them because they help ensure that guests will reply promptly.

Map or directions—If a map or directions to the wedding and/or reception are needed, they should be included in the invitation package. It looks much better if the map is professionally drawn and the map and/or directions are printed in the same color ink and on the same card stock as the invitation. Alternatively, use a map photocopied on fine-quality paper. A beautifully printed invitation is undercut by a poor-quality map or amateurishly written directions.

Rehearsal dinner invitation—If the rehearsal dinner is being given by the same individuals who are hosting the wedding, an invitation insert may be sent in the same package as the wedding invitation. Or, if a casual rehearsal dinner is planned—a Southern-style barbecue, or a clambake— a less formal invitation can be mailed three weeks before the event. Often, the rehearsal dinner is hosted by another individual or family, and in such a case the invitation could be sent by them directly and need not reflect the style of the wedding invitation.

Wedding announcement—Wedding announcements are mailed the day after the wedding to acquaintances who were not invited to the wedding.

Ceremony program—Consider ordering extra folded blank programs in your paper stock so that the program at your church, synagogue, or other ceremony site can be printed on the stock to continue the style of your invitation.

Menu—You might want to consider ordering blank paper stock that matches your invitation to use for menus that will be printed or lettered in calligraphy later.

Thank-you notes—These can be printed at the same time as the invitations and may reflect the style of the invitations or not, as you prefer. Again, depending on preference a simple "Thank you" or the bride's or couple's names or monogram may be preprinted on the stock. Never, never use the "fill-in-the-blank" style of thank-you note—"Thank you for the _____ ." This is the height of bad taste and poor manners. It takes just a few minutes to hand-write a proper thank-you note. Your guests spend a great deal of thought, time, and money on your wedding gift; they deserve as much consideration.

Personal stationery—If the bride has elected to take her husband's name, or if the couple is moving to a new residence, this is also the ideal time to have personal stationery printed.

INVITATION WORDING

Wording for wedding invitations is more complex than in the past. Traditionally, the wedding invitation followed a standard format: the parents of the bride invited guests to the wedding of their daughter. Times have changed. Today, the bride and groom may be holding the wedding and inviting the guests. Perhaps the groom's family is cohosting the wedding with the bride's family. Divorces and remarriages in the bride's or groom's family call for careful phrasing. A skilled wedding specialist at your stationery store should be able to assist you in phrasing your invitation so that it reads well and is appropriate for your family situation.

In formal invitations, the British spelling of words such as "honour" and "favour" is often used. For ceremonies in a house of worship, the invitation requests "the honour of your presence." For ceremonies in a secular setting, the invitation requests "the pleasure of your company."

Whether or not you choose to follow these traditions is entirely up to you.

SAMPLE INVITATION WORDING

Traditional style: This style of invitation is appropriate for a formal wedding in a house of worship with a reception at another location.

Mr. and Mrs. James M. Morris
request the honour of your presence
at the marriage of their daughter
Janice Adams
to
Mr. George Scott Matthews III
on Saturday, the seventh of June
Nineteen hundred and ninety-seven
at five o'clock
First Presbyterian Church
120 Ledge Road
Los Angeles, California
Reception to follow
Hotel Bel-Air
100 Stone Canyon Road
Los Angeles

This style of invitation is appropriate when the bride and groom are hosting their own wedding.

Ruth Anne Atkins and George Steven Weinstock III
request the honor of your presence
at the celebration of their marriage
on Saturday, the seventh of June
Nineteen hundred and ninety-seven
at five o'clock
Temple Beth Israel
320 Blackstone Boulevard
Providence, Rhode Island
Reception following
The Statler Hotel
or
The honor of your presence
is requested at the marriage of
Ms. Ruth Anne Atkins
to
Mr. George Steven Weinstock III
etc.

Kate Edelman and Deane Johnson
request the pleasure of your company
as they join in marriage
Saturday, the twelfth of October
at six o'clock
1017 Ridgedale Drive
Beverly Hills

Black tie

This wording is appropriate when the divorced parents of the bride are inviting guests to a ceremony and reception held at the same location. Placing the parents' names on separate lines and not linking them with the word "and" signifies a divorce.

Mrs. Eliza S. Bedell
Mr. John T. Bedell
request the pleasure of your company
at the marriage of their daughter
Patricia Scott
to
Mr. Ralph Monson Harwood
Saturday, the seventh of June
Nineteen hundred and ninety-seven
at five o'clock
Lakeside Country Club
200 River Road
Chicago, Illinois
and afterward at the reception

This style of invitation is appropriate when the two families wish both sets of parents to be mentioned on the invitation.

Mr. and Mrs. William Keller Cox
request the pleasure of your company
at the marriage of their daughter
Harriet Grant
to
Mr. Michael Pratt McDonald
son of Dr. and Mrs. Mark Francis McDonald
on Saturday, the seventh of June
Nineteen hundred and ninety-seven
at five o'clock
in the garden
320 Georgica Road
East Hampton, New York

This style of invitation is appropriate for an informal wedding hosted by the bride's parents, with the ceremony and reception at home.

Mr. and Mrs. Julius Sanders Richardson
request the pleasure of your company
at the marriage of their daughter
Alicia Rose
to
Mr. Ralph Monson Harwood
Saturday, the seventh of June
Nineteen hundred and ninety-seven
at five o'clock
in the garden
720 Tamarack Road
Naples, Florida
and afterward at the reception

INVITATION ACCENTS

You can transform a simple invitation into a more personal statement by adding a design accent. It gives the invitation an individual look and can be a beautiful way to tie in the theme or color scheme of your wedding. Many of these ideas are simple and can be done at home.

• Use satin ribbon to fasten reply cards and envelopes to one panel of your invitation
• Seal the invitation with sealing wax and a monogram or icon
• Include a dried flower pressed between two sheets of tissue
• Wrap the invitation with ribbon that matches your wedding colors
• Use sheer, handmade paper or rice paper instead of a tissue insert

This style of invitation is appropriate for an informal wedding hosted by the bride and groom with the ceremony and reception at the same site.

Sandra and Peter
request the pleasure of your company
at the celebration of their marriage
on Saturday, the seventh of June
at five o'clock
Circle Bar Ranch
500 River Road
Sun Valley, Idaho
Reception following

Another approach that is informal and very personal is to send the wedding invitation in the form of a letter. A beautiful way to do this is to have a calligrapher write the letter of invitation in elegant script, and then have it printed:

Dear_____,

We are getting married on Saturday the 15th of May and would love for you to share in our celebration. The ceremony will be held at the Bay Club, Southampton, at 4 o'clock in the afternoon, with a reception to follow. We hope you can join us.

Much love,
Karen and Gordon

The calligrapher hand-letters each invitee's name in the space after the salutation, making each invitation look as though it were personally scripted.

Invitations should be addressed to the specific guest or guests who are invited. If children are invited, their names should be included in the address along with those of their parents. If you are inviting an unmarried guest and would like to encourage him or her to bring a date, add the words "and guest" to the name on the address. If you are using a calligrapher or if someone else is hand-addressing your invitation envelopes, be sure the list you give them is worded exactly the way you want the envelope to read. It's not the calligrapher's responsibility to make judgment calls on salutations, titles, names, and addresses.

One question I am frequently asked is whether it is ever proper to include in the invitation a list of preferred wedding gifts or a list of the stores where the bride and groom are registered for gifts. The answer is no. An invitation to a wedding asks guests to share in a joyous celebration; it is not a solicitation for gifts. Thoughtful guests who want to give an appropriate wedding gift will inquire where the bridal couple is registered.

THE WELCOME PACKAGE

If you have many guests who are traveling to your wedding from out of town, it is thoughtful to prepare a welcome package that is left for them at the hotel registration desk or placed in their preassigned room. The welcome package is designed to show guests how grateful you are that they have traveled to share in your celebration, and to provide a reminder of the schedule of events that relate to your wedding. By providing all the information in one place, the welcome package helps guests be more self-sufficient, and means that the bride and groom needn't worry about filling guests' off-hours.

The most important component of the welcome package is a note from the bride and groom thanking the guest for traveling to the ceremony. The note or an attached schedule should provide a reminder of the ceremony time and location, and information about any other events to be held before or after the wedding—scheduling, attire recommendations, local temperatures and weather conditions, maps, etc. The package should also provide a name and local phone number of someone to speak with should guests need further information or assistance. I advise against including the bride as the contact person; instead, include a number for the wedding consultant, a travel planner, or a friend who is helping with your wedding.

A welcome package might also include a package of touristic information (some of which may be obtained from the local chamber of commerce or tourist authority), including current shows at local museums, popular movies, sporting events, restaurant recommendations, art galleries, and other pastimes you enjoy and would like to share with your guests.

Even if you are just providing a note and a schedule, present them in a special way. Tie the note with a beautiful piece of satin ribbon and fasten it to a scented candle. Roll the note into a scroll, fasten it with raffia, and attach dried flowers and cinnamon sticks. Taking the time to add that special touch shows your guests how much you appreciate their presence at your celebration.

While it is by no means necessary, creating a welcoming gift for your guests who are traveling from out of town is a thoughtful gesture. If you are having a country wedding, nestle your welcome note in a rustic basket that holds fresh seasonal fruit. If your wedding is contemporary in style, you might obtain plain cardboard boxes, line them with tissue paper, and fill each with your welcome note, a fragrant candle, and a relaxing eye mask. For a midsummer wedding by the sea, it's a fun idea to take a canvas bag and, in addition to a note from the bride and groom, fill it with beach gear such as suntan lotion, a sun visor, fruit, and a big bottle of water.

Other components of a welcome gift basket might include (either singly or in combination):
- Fine chocolates
- Bath salts, bubble bath, or other bath products
- Wine or champagne
- Mineral water
- Flowers
- Fresh fruit, such as two green apples, or a bunch of ripe grapes
- Cheese
- Freshly baked cookies

W

hen I ask brides what moved them most about their wedding, almost invariably they recall a moment during the ceremony. One bride told me she was brought to tears during the recitation of her vows, when she looked across at her groom, and noticed *his* eyes were moist. Another bride confessed that she was "perfectly fine" during the ceremony until her maid of honor, a gifted soprano, stepped forward to sing the bride's favorite hymn. "I just couldn't keep the tears from my eyes, remembering how long we have been friends," she explained.

The wedding ceremony marks a turning point in your life. It should be exactly the way you and your fiancé want it to be. It should be uniquely yours.

With all the attention paid to the other elements in a typical wedding, the ceremony often receives less attention than it rightfully deserves. Many couples breeze through plans for the ceremony without much thought or creativity. Perhaps they add a favorite hymn, or delete antiquated wording from traditional vows. But by and large, the standard ceremony goes unquestioned.

My view is that your wedding ceremony should fit your values and personality—fit you as perfectly as your wedding dress. Your wedding ritual might be a five-minute civil ceremony, a spiritual ceremony with a meaningful reading by you and your groom, or a traditional church service full of pomp and circumstance. It may take place in a cathedral or on a boat. Whatever you choose, it should be an expression of you and your groom.

If you and your fiancé are from the same religious and social background, you may easily agree on a traditional approach to the ceremony. But that situation occurs less and less frequently. Today, there are more interracial, interfaith, and intercultural marriages than ever before. Because of this, many couples are opting for a less religious and more spiritual feeling at their ceremony.

Ceremonies generally fall into one of four major categories:
•Religious: Imbued with the beliefs and rituals of a particular faith, the ceremony is performed by a priest, minister, rabbi, or other ordained official.
•Interfaith: When individuals of different faiths are joined in marriage, the ceremony may be performed by two officiants, one from each faith, or by one officiant who is familiar with both religions.
•Secular or civil: In a civil service, a judge officiates, using a nonsectarian text.
•Spiritual: Increasingly popular, spiritual ceremonies emphasize humanistic values rather than a religious belief system.

Within each major category, there is plenty of flexibility to incorporate elements that express your personalities and values. Customize your ceremony by writing your own vows, asking friends to give readings, incorporating poetry or music, or involving your nieces and nephews.

The officiant—minister, priest, rabbi, judge—can also help you create a personalized ceremony. The choice of officiant is an extremely important one. Be sure you have a rapport with him or her. Well in advance, meet to discuss what you desire in your ceremony. Listen to the officiant's suggestions and see if he or she seems responsive to your plans. Be sure to ask to read what he or she intends to say during the ceremony. Find out how long the standard ceremony is. State your opinions. Make changes, additions, or deletions. It's perfectly acceptable to interview

several prospective officiants so that you can find the one with whom you feel most comfortable.

Your lifestyle, family background, and personal taste will dictate the type of ceremony that is best for you. Will it be traditional, with a full complement of bridesmaids and groomsmen and arranged according to time-honored rituals? Or will it be nontraditional, with no attendants but with the bride coming down the aisle alone or escorted by her husband-to-be? The melding of different beliefs and backgrounds into a personal ceremony makes for a truly meaningful occasion. Creating an interfaith ceremony, perhaps with two officiants, can be a rewarding experience that brings a couple and their families closer together. Be aware, however, that some officiants and congregations do not permit outside clergy or may have restrictions that prohibit an interfaith ceremony. This is one of the reasons it is so important to discuss your plans in detail with your officiant.

Remember that ultimately, you are in charge of your wedding ritual. If you are dealing with a church or temple where the officiant is inflexible and has many rules that are preventing you from creating the ceremony that you wish, perhaps you should consider holding your ceremony else-where. Don't be forced into a ceremony that doesn't feel right, just because "it's the way we've always done it here."

THE CEREMONY SETTING

The place where your ceremony will be held can also influence the style and type of ceremony you choose. If you have long dreamed of an intimate candlelit wedding in a tiny, wooden country chapel, then your ceremony should be simple, to suit the surroundings. If you intend to marry in the temple of your groom's family, your ceremony will probably be structured according to Jewish traditions, but it can still incorporate your wishes and preferences.

Keep in mind that every wedding ceremony needs a spiritual center, a visual focal point. In a church or synagogue, the focal point is the altar. In other locations, you can create a spiritual center where your ceremony will take place, accenting it visually with a floral arch or trellis, large urns filled with topiaries, a pair of pedestals, or swags of greenery and flowers—there is no limit. Look creatively at your venue to determine the best place to hold your ceremony. If you are in a hotel space, don't automatically choose the spot where ceremonies are usually held; there may be another configuration that will work better for you.

In any ceremony, it is important to create a sense of intimacy. If you are in a temple that seats 300 and you have 125 guests, you should encourage all the guests to sit at the front. This can be done by illuminating and decorating only the area where you want people to sit, or by roping off pews that you want to keep off-limits. If you have ushers, they can direct guests to pews at the front.

You can heighten the impact of your ceremony by having events unfold in a dramatic manner. A choir walking down the aisle of a church, one by one, singing a glorious hymn, is a moving way to open a wedding service. Flower girls strewing a thick carpet of rose petals in the aisle adds beauty to the procession and builds anticipation for the bride's entrance. The recitation of a poem that has meaning to the bridal couple gives an emotional aspect to the ceremony. Drama can also be heightened by using candles as lighting for your ceremony.

VIDEOTAPING AND PHOTOGRAPHING THE CEREMONY

Many bridal couples have their ceremony photographed, and many have the ceremony videotaped. When you are working with a photographer or videographer, it is important to set ground rules in advance. I believe it is unwise to attempt to document every moment of the ceremony on film or video. I have heard of weddings where the video production looked to the guests like a small movie set. Unless you are broadcasting your ceremony live, there is no need to have elaborate video production! The idea is to capture some of the most meaningful moments on film and video without intruding on the ceremony.

Camera work should be unobtrusive. A skilled camera operator can get the footage needed without distracting the guests from your ceremony. The camera operators should take care to stay to the side so as not to obstruct guests' views. Lighting should be kept to a minimum. If lighting is necessary, be sure that it is never switched on abruptly, but shielded and gradually allowed to illuminate the area.

SOUND

Microphones make some brides and grooms uncomfortable, but it is important that your ceremony be audible to your guests. An outdoor field makes a lovely setting for a wedding, but if the wind is blowing the wrong way, no one will be able to hear a word that is spoken by the officiant, bride, or groom.

I recommend microphones for all but the smallest weddings. You can choose between a standup mike, or lavalier microphones that are attached to the clothing of the bridal party. If you use lavaliers, it usually suffices to have the groom and the officiant wear the microphones. Attaching a lavalier mike to a bridal gown can be challenging, and normally the groom's lavalier is adequate to pick up the bride's responses.

The key thing to remember with audio equipment is to do a careful sound check prior to the ceremony to make sure all the equipment is working properly and that the sound is at the right level for all areas of your venue.

REFRESHING DRINKS BEFORE THE CEREMONY

When guests arrive at the ceremony venue, pass light, refreshing nonalcoholic drinks, and make them visually appealing by serving them in wineglasses garnished with fresh mint or lemon peel. Unless the ceremony is very short, avoid serving alcohol to guests beforehand. An alcoholic drink right before the ceremony and at the start of a long evening fatigues guests. Different drink options include:

Iced tea with fresh mint sprig

- Fresh lemonade, or club soda and lemonade, with a sprig of mint
- Fresh lemonade with a sprig of lavender or rosemary
- Sparkling water with a slice of lemon or lime
- A combination of half iced tea and half lemonade with a sprig of mint
- Flavored teas with a fresh berry as garnish
- Juice coolers made with one third fruit juice (raspberry, cranberry, or passion fruit) and two thirds sparkling water, garnished with a fresh berry or fruit slice
- Sparkling water with Rose's lime juice and a sprig of mint

The ceremony can be a wonderful opportunity to involve the people who are most important in your life. Think about the strengths and talents of the people who are closest to you and how they might participate in your ceremony. You could ask a friend who writes poetry to read a love poem at your ceremony. Your cousin with the beautiful voice might perform a solo aria.

Don't hesitate to propose a change in the standard approach. One ceremony uniting a pair of classical music lovers began, as guests were being seated, with a solo violinist playing on a raised dais, silhouetted behind a diaphanous scrim of chiffon. The solo violinist was joined by a second violinist who took his place on the dais and began to play. One by one, the chamber orchestra swelled to a dozen stringed instruments. When all the musicians were assembled, the scrim was raised, and the ceremony began with the entrance of the groom, his groomsmen, and the minister. It was a dramatic way to open the wedding ritual.

One bride I worked with wanted to have many of her close friends involved in her ceremony but didn't want formal bridesmaids. Before the ceremony, a dozen selected guests were given a beautiful flower. After the bride walked down the aisle, the selected guests rose and, one by one, walked to the chuppah and handed her a flower. When the bride's arms were full of beautiful blossoms, her mother tied them together with an ivory French silk ribbon, making a simple bouquet that the bride held throughout the ceremony. It was an unusual ritual that symbolized her close ties to her supportive, devoted friends. And it was completely original.

Another couple who shared a love of opera wanted to incorporate a favorite aria into their ceremony. Their wedding began with a prelude of opera overtures played by a chamber orchestra as family and friends took their seats in the church. Instead of a traditional procession of family members and attendants, the bride and groom walked down the aisle together, and each sat with his or her respective families. Then, a soprano dressed in dark blue satin stepped onto the dais to sing Caccini's "Ave Maria." When the aria ended, you could have heard a pin drop in the church. The singer gave a slight bow and walked off the dais; the minister stepped forward and asked the bride and groom to join him at the altar. Opening the ceremony with this compelling piece of music gave the ritual a feeling of solemnness and grace.

One of my most memorable moments was the wedding ceremony of Kenny G to Lyndie Benson. Kenny wrote the lovely melody entitled "The Wedding Song," which played as Lyndie walked down the aisle. It was the most beautiful song. I clearly remember seeing tears in not only the guests' eyes but also in the eyes of many of the waitstaff.

An evening ceremony that I found particularly moving incorporated an inspiring symbolic element, the unity candle. Each guest received an unlit candle upon entering the ceremony site. At the beginning of the ceremony, while beautiful music played in the background, the bride and groom each took a lit taper and together lit a unity candle. Then, the bride and groom walked to each row of guests and lit the candle of the guest on the end of the row. That candle then lit the candle of the next guest, and so on. Soon, the entire space was bathed in the flickering glow of 125 candles. The effect was enchanting. After the ceremony, the candles were placed into a large sandbox outside the ceremony area, where they burned with a soft radiance for hours.

Perhaps you want an even more personal, intimate ceremony. One engaged couple who never felt comfortable at big parties decided to take another approach. They selected a beautiful spot on a high bluff

EXPLAINING THE CEREMONY

For interfaith weddings, or for religious ceremonies attended by guests who are not of the same faith, consider creating a small scroll or card that describes the rituals and customs of the wedding ceremony in each of the bride's and groom's religions. This helps guests understand and appreciate the nuances of the wedding ritual. The card can be rolled and tied with a ribbon, or kept flat and decorated with a dried flower glued to the top of the page. The ceremony cards can be placed on each seat, handed to guests as they enter the ceremony area, or placed in baskets for guests to take while enjoying pre-ceremony refreshments.

THE CEREMONY PROGRAM

Many churches and synagogues provide a standardized printed program for weddings. If you create your own program, you can include basic information, such as the names of hymns and readings, while adding your own personal touches. If you will be printing your program, use a good quality card stock that matches the style of your invitation. In addition to listing the ceremony elements, your program might include the names of those in the bridal party, and the full text of readings, songs, or hymns. Families can also honor absent or departed loved ones with a dedication on the back page.

THE CHUPPAH

In the Jewish wedding ceremony, the bride, groom, and their parents stand under a chuppah, or wedding canopy, while the vows are taken. The chuppah symbolizes the new home of the bride and groom. Traditionally, the chuppah was a tallis (prayer shawl) fastened to the ends of four poles or broomsticks. Today, a chuppah can be made of flowers, fabric—anything that symbolizes shelter. If you use a tallis, it can be pinned or stitched to the underside of a larger piece of fabric to make a more spacious canopy. Chuppah poles may be elaborately painted or gilded, garlanded with ivy or leaves, or topped with tassels. A beautiful stationary chuppah can be made by placing the poles into four large terra-cotta pots planted with flowers, topping the poles with a trellis, and adorning it with vines and flowers.

overlooking the ocean. Just before dawn on a summer weekday morning, a small group—the bride and groom, a justice of the peace, the couple's two best friends, and a photographer—met at the spot. As the sun rose, the bride, dressed in a simple white chiffon slip dress cut on the bias and carrying a nosegay of creamy ranunculus, and the groom, attired in an ivory linen suit, recited their vows. The photographer unobtrusively captured the significant moments of the simple ceremony in this breathtakingly beautiful setting. After the ceremony, the wedding party retired to a comfortable suite at a nearby inn overlooking the ocean to enjoy cappuccino and a basket of home-baked muffins. At nine A.M., the bridal party welcomed sixteen family members and friends to the inn for a festive wedding breakfast on the open-air patio. It was a very personal, joyful celebration that suited this couple perfectly.

Many brides and grooms today want a minimal wedding ceremony, a brief, five-minute ritual, and then a great party. In this situation, an approach that works well is to delay the ceremony rather than holding it as soon as guests are assembled. When guests arrive, they can enjoy a cocktail reception. Then, the ceremony occurs, and after that dinner follows immediately. By delaying the ceremony and creating anticipation, you can impart a sense of occasion to a ritual that otherwise might seem too brief.

One couple who had lived together for several years didn't feel a typical wedding was appropriate for them. Since they had a well-established household, they particularly didn't want their family and friends to shower them with wedding presents. So they outsmarted everyone. They invited a hundred close friends and family members to a fabulous summer garden party. Their house was filled with beautiful arrangements of vibrant pink cosmos, asters, and peonies from their garden. The champagne flowed like water.

A half hour into the party, the groom signaled for attention. "I have a little announcement to make," he said. "I have asked you all here for a reason. You are the nearest and dearest people to our hearts, and Ellen and I want you to witness our marriage." As the delighted guests applauded, a justice of the peace took his place beside the groom, and the bride's mother began to play the couple's grand piano in an adjoining room. Ellen entered wearing a simple dress in pale pink silk, and carrying an arm bouquet of fuchsia cosmos from the garden. A brief ceremony was followed by an evening of celebrating among family and friends, who to this day are still amazed that the bride and groom were able to pull off such a coup.

Why not plan a weekend away with friends instead of a traditional wedding? Two friends of mine both had been married once before and didn't want a large reception. He did a little research and found a great resort on the beach in Mexico that had about a dozen very inexpensive bungalows. He, his bride, and ten other couples flew to Mexico to spend a glorious long weekend at this resort.

The celebration began on Friday night with margaritas and a barbecue on the property. On Saturday, everyone did as he or she wished; some went fishing, while others explored the little resort town. Later that day, as the sun was setting over the Pacific, everyone gathered on the beach around a huge bonfire to witness a wedding ceremony that was officiated by the local judge. Toasts were made with a magnum of champagne that had been carefully hand-carried on the plane. Later, the coals of the bonfire were used to cook part of the wedding feast. The dinner, which was catered by the resort, included corn on the cob and whole fish, both roasted over the coals and served with tomatillo and mango salsas;

grilled shrimp with fresh lime juice; handmade tortillas, black beans and rice; and lots of ice-cold Mexican beer.

The feast culminated with the cutting of a single-layer lemon-walnut cake from the bride's favorite bakery, another item that had been hand-carried on the plane. The square cake was frosted plainly and unadorned except for a vintage porcelain bride and groom cake topper—an heirloom handed down in the bride's family. The cake was served with spoonfuls of mango ice cream purchased from a shop in the local village. Toward the end of the evening, guests sat on the beach and chatted quietly as the moonlight illuminated the waves. No one who attended this unusual wedding will ever forget the fun and togetherness of the weekend away with a dozen close friends.

MUSIC

Music is a key element in the wedding ceremony because it creates a mood, expresses your feelings of love and joy on your wedding day, and controls the energy of your ceremony.

Typically, ceremonies call for several different moods of music. As guests begin to arrive, prelude music sets the stage for the ceremony. It is important to plan to have music playing even before guests enter the ceremony area. You never want guests entering a space that is silent. The right prelude music draws people into an environment and makes them feel welcome. Prelude music may last anywhere from twenty minutes to a half hour or more, and is generally a tranquil style of music that plays in the background as guests are seated.

Processional music changes the mood. It is designed to create a sense of anticipation as the wedding party enters the ceremony space, and builds up to the bride's entrance. Unless the aisle at your venue is very long, it's best to have one piece of music during the entrance of the wedding party and another for the bride. If the music changes frequently during the procession, the effect is choppy rather than harmonious. When it is time for the entrance of the bride, there should be either a change of music or a natural pause in the music, and the volume should be turned up a notch, to heighten the feeling of anticipation. I advise brides

LIVE MUSIC OPTIONS FOR THE CEREMONY

Church organ

Piano

Solo violin

String trio (violin, viola, and cello) or quartet (two violins, viola, and cello)

Piano trio (piano, violin, and cello) or piano quartet (piano, violin, viola, and cello)

Flute and keyboard

Guitar, cello, and flute

Gospel choir

Vocalist

Harp

Harp and flute

Wind trio or quartet (assorted wind instruments, depending on the music, such as clarinet, oboe, flute, trumpet, French horn, or bassoon)

Chamber music ensemble (a small orchestra with strings, wind instruments, and percussion)

Church choir

Children's choir

Classical guitar

that once the bridal music begins, they should count to ten slowly before making an entrance, adding another element of drama to the ceremony.

During the ceremony itself, there is a variety of musical pieces you might select depending on the mood you are trying to create. Any musical piece that is meaningful to you can be incorporated into your service—although if you are being married at a house of worship, you should check to see if there are restrictions about music. Don't fall back on the standard wedding music unless it truly speaks to you. If you want to hire a gospel choir, to sing spirituals, or hear your favorite rock ballad, it's your choice. Other options include hymns (sung by a soloist, choir, or the congregation), songs or arias, classical pieces, or popular music selections.

Finally, there is recessional music, which is generally upbeat and joyous to celebrate the bride and groom and accompany the wedding party's walk down the aisle. Turn the volume up to enhance the joy of the moment and keep the music playing until the last guest has left the ceremony area.

Your ceremony could feature live or recorded music, or a combination of the two. Some brides dream of walking down the aisle to a specific song by a favorite artist and so choose a recording. Others prefer the immediacy and intimacy of live music.

The challenge with using recorded music is timing. The procession down the aisle should be rehearsed with the exact musical selection, ensuring that it doesn't end until the procession is complete. Check the TRT (total running time) on the disc or cassette and monitor it carefully. It doesn't matter if the song continues after the bride has reached the altar, but if the song ends when she's three quarters of the way down the aisle, it's awkward. If you are using several recordings during the ceremony, each piece should be on a separate cassette tape or CD and queued up so that it can be changed quickly.

Of course, live music has more impact than recorded music. Many of the most powerful moments at wedding ceremonies occur with a particularly moving piece played by a musician, or a song sung by a vocalist or choir. Using live music at the ceremony may actually be easier than using recordings, because musicians can respond to the speed of the procession and extend or shorten their playing as necessary.

Unless a long ceremony is dictated by your religious or cultural background, don't protract it. If one or more elements drag on too long, guests become distracted. A short and tightly orchestrated ceremony of no more than twenty minutes is more enjoyable and memorable. If you do plan a long ceremony, keep the energy moving with ritual music or songs.

REHEARSING THE CEREMONY

Unless you are having a very simple five-minute ceremony, you should plan on a rehearsal involving everyone in the wedding party. Note that it is not always possible to have the officiant at the rehearsal, although it is preferable. The rehearsal usually takes place the day or evening before the wedding, and traditionally is followed by a rehearsal dinner.

When everyone is assembled at the site, begin by pointing out where they are to stand at the altar, chuppah, or ceremony focal point. Sometimes marking the floor with colored masking tape is helpful, particularly in planning where the wedding party will stand for photos. This will save time during the actual photo session.

Walk through the procession, ceremony, and recession. Make sure you have the ceremony music in order to practice the walk down the aisle to ensure the pieces are the appropriate length. Depending on how complex your ceremony is, you may have to rehearse it two, three, or more times until everyone is comfortable with his or her role. It is a very good idea to include any children in the wedding party so that they can become comfortable with what is expected of them. Make sure everyone understands who is in front of and behind them during the procession. Finally, be sure to tell everyone the exact time and place to meet the following day.

THE CEREMONY FLOURISH

At the conclusion of the ceremony, consider a dramatic touch—or even a bit of fun—to kick off the celebration. When it was time for her recessional, Holly Robinson arranged for the entire USC marching band to parade smartly up the aisle and right past her astonished husband—to everyone's delight.

One bride who was marrying a man of Scottish descent honored his heritage by arranging for a bagpiper, dressed in the groom's family tartan, to stand at the door of the church and begin playing his bagpipes right after the bride and groom had kissed. Like the Pied Piper, the bagpiper led a procession of the newlyweds, wedding party, and guests to the reception, playing Scottish airs every step of the way.

Think of the fun when the gospel choir that has sung hymns throughout the service suddenly breaks into a great, hand-clapping song like "Oh Happy Day" for the recessional. Other ideas? After the bride and groom kiss, have attendants toss showers of rose petals from an overhead balcony, have a fountain erupt with a stream of water, or arrange for the simultaneous popping of a dozen champagne corks.

THE REHEARSAL

Arrange for the following items to be at the ceremony site for the rehearsal:
• All the ceremony music, so that the length of the music may be coordinated with the processions and other ceremony elements
• Any electronic or sound equipment needed to play recordings or amplify sound
• Text of readings
• Refreshments, glasses and cocktail napkins
• Colored masking tape for marking the floor, if necessary

REHEARSAL BOUQUET

One lovely custom is for the bride to fashion a "bouquet" from all the ribbons on gifts she received at the shower and before the wedding. She then uses this brightly colored ribbon bouquet when she walks down the aisle at the rehearsal.

THE BREAKING OF THE GLASS

In the traditional Jewish wedding ceremony, after the bride and groom have been announced as husband and wife, the groom places a napkin-wrapped glass on the floor and steps firmly on it, breaking the glass. The symbolism of this act is the subject of much discussion, but most agree that it reminds us of the joy, sorrow, and fragility of life. A suggestion: instead of a glass, use a light bulb secured in a sturdy zip-top plastic bag and wrapped in a napkin. It makes a satisfying shattering noise with no danger of injury.

SEATING AT THE CEREMONY

If you have seating for guests at your ceremony, consider whether you want an area or areas reserved for family. With a small wedding, assigned seating may be unnecessary, but with a larger wedding, it is thoughtful to make special seating arrangements for elderly guests, and to preplan seating to avoid any awkwardness caused by divorces or interfamily problems. Use assigned seating cards that are printed with guests' names and placed on the pew or chair backs. The seating cards should be attractively designed and either hand-lettered or printed on a personal computer. With assigned seating, you will need the groomsmen or ushers to escort guests to the proper seats, so be sure to provide them with a seating chart. It is best to have just a few assigned seats rather than to plan seating for a large portion of the guests.

THE KEEPSAKE NOTE

One custom that I like very much is to have note cards and envelopes on the guest book table, along with a little sign asking guests to write a note of congratulations, reminiscences, or other thoughts to the bride and groom. These may be collected or dropped into a basket at the reception. The bride and groom save these notes and open them on their first anniversary.

DEALING WITH VENDORS

Be sure your directions to the vendors—florist, caterer, musicians, setup crew—are explicit and well understood. For example: a wedding was to feature a talented flautist playing for the bride's entrance. The flautist failed to show up. At the last minute, there was a scramble to locate appropriate recorded wedding music and a portable cassette player on which to play it. Fortunately, someone had a tape of "The Wedding Song" by Kenny G; a cassette player was found; and the bride made her entrance on time. Postscript: the flautist had arrived punctually, but she went to another wedding taking place just up the road at the same time!

CEREMONY MUSIC FAVORITES

Classical Piece

Classical Piece	Composer
"Arioso"	Bach
"Ave Maria"	Schubert
"Wedding March" from *Lohengrin*	Wagner
Brandenburg Concertos	Bach
Canon in D Minor	Pachelbel
"Coronation March"	Walton
"Jesu, Joy of Man's Desiring"	Bach
"Love Theme" from *Romeo & Juliet*	Tchaikovsky
"Musetta's Waltz" from *La Bohème*	Puccini
"Ode to Joy" from Symphony No. 9	Beethoven
"Pomp and Circumstance No. 4"	Elgar
"O mio babbino caro" from *Gianni Schicchi*	Puccini
Romance No. 2 in F	Beethoven
"Save the Best for Last"	Vaughan Williams
"Spring" from *The Four Seasons*	Vivaldi
"Trumpet Voluntary"	Clarke
"Waltz"	Strauss
Water Music	Handel
"Wedding March" from *A Midsummer Night's Dream*	Mendelssohn

Jewish Traditional Songs

"Dodi Li"	Traditional
"Erev Shel Shoshanim"	Traditional
"Siman Tov"	Traditional
"Mazel Tov"	Traditional

Standards

"Isn't It Romantic"	Hart /Rodgers
"One Hand, One Heart"	Sondheim/Bernstein
"Someone to Watch Over Me"	Gershwin
"Summertime"	Heyward/Gershwin
"Sunrise Sunset"	Harnick /Bock

Contemporary Favorites

"All I Ask of You"	Webber
"Evergreen"	Streisand
"Somewhere in Time"	Barry
"Somewhere Out There"	Horner
"The Wedding Song"	Kenny G

edding planners will tell you how often they meet with a bride for the first time to discuss her wedding, only to find she already owns the wedding dress. Yet she has no idea what the style of her wedding will be, or where and at what time of day it will be held. Too often, as plans for the wedding evolve, the dress turns out to be a mistake. It is overly formal for an afternoon ceremony, or the wrong style for the reception at the location that has been chosen.

The bride's dress and the groom's attire are both part of the big picture of the wedding. The bride and groom should be dressed appropriately for the style and type of wedding, time of day, season of the year, and location of the event. I always advise brides to buy their wedding dress after they have determined the basic elements of their wedding.

Your wedding dress, like your wedding itself, is your personal expression—not your mother's, or your maid of honor's, or your fiancé's. You, the bride, are the center of attention at your wedding, and you will be looking at wedding photos of yourself for decades to come. It is very important that you are completely satisfied with your dress.

I frequently meet brides who were coaxed into a dress by their mother, a close friend, or an overeager salesperson. Inevitably, the dress becomes a source of tension as the bride agonizes about replacing it versus getting married in a dress she doesn't like.

Don't buy a dress because your mother thinks it's *perfect,* or because you feel pressured by salespeople who threaten that if you don't order that day, you won't get your dress in time for the wedding. That's nonsense. Take your time, do your homework, and you'll find the dress that's right for you.

Start by keeping a file of pictures from magazines. Magazines are a great source of ideas as you plan your wedding outfit. Don't limit your research to bridal magazines; peruse fashion magazines as well. Save as many photos as you can of the dresses you like and take them with you when you shop. With pictures in hand, you'll be able to give the sales staff better direction and the shopping will take less time.

The leading designers have trunk shows that travel from city to city. Watch for these, because they are great opportunities to see the most current wedding dress designs. Trunk shows are typically held in the winter and fall. Bridal shops will alert you to forthcoming shows if you register with them.

I advise brides who are shopping for a gown to go to at least three different stores and try on as many different dresses as possible before buying one. I know—to many women that sounds like a lot of work. But it's important to try on a range of styles so that you can determine what really looks good on you. Examine the line of the dress. Be sure you have plenty of space in the fitting room to see how you look from afar. And keep an open mind. Often a dress looks terrible hanging on a rack, but it absolutely transforms you when it's on your body.

While most bridal salon salespeople will usher you directly to a rack of elaborate gowns, many women look much better in a simpler dress that suits the surroundings at their wedding. A small wedding at home may be an occasion for an understated dress or two-piece suit that fits the intimate setting. An outdoor wedding under a tent in July might call for a strappy A-line, or a simple fitted dress of crisp linen. If your reception is to be held in an ornately decorated hotel ballroom, a more formal

dress, perhaps with a train and veil, may be appropriate. For a grand church wedding, you can wear an elaborate gown with a cathedral-length train, veil, and gloves. Just remember to consider the big picture when you think about your dress.

Of course, the big picture also means the budget. When you plan your overall wedding budget, be realistic about how much money is appropriate to spend on your attire. Rushing out to buy the dress before the wedding has been planned may cause you to spend more than is prudent. Remember that the dress is just one piece of the picture. Rather than overextending your budget on your dress, choose an appropriately priced outfit and spend your money on a great party.

Thankfully, the whole approach to wedding dresses has changed. The bridal industry has become much more fashion-conscious, and today it is acceptable for brides to select a dress from a favorite fashion designer or boutique rather than a bridal shop. Brides don't have to feel locked into a traditional bridal gown if their style is more natural or avant-garde.

Many of the world's leading couturiers have created their own signature bridal collections that show alternative gowns. The basic look today is pure and simple. A-line is extremely popular, and shades of off-white and pastels are seen in addition to traditional white and ivory.

My philosophy has always been that less is more when it comes to bridal gowns. I am not enamored of elaborate dresses that are made of multiple fabrics and are heavily ornamented. The best effect is when a wedding dress is composed of preferably one, or a maximum of two fabrics. Some of my favorite fabrics include silk dupioni, duchesse satin, silk organza, four-ply silk, charmeuse, pleated tulle, and silk tulle. By working with just one or two of these fabrics, you can create a simple and beautiful look. A dress that combines many fabrics, textures, and decorative elements can look fussy. Remember that it's not just the dress; there may be a veil or headpiece; there will be shoes, jewelry, maybe gloves, and, of course, the bouquet. It is very easy to look overproduced. If you are not conscious of all the elements, the dress may end up wearing the bride, rather than the other way around.

In planning your wedding attire, consider the season of the year and the colors and fabrics that are most appropriate. Spring and summer are the times for soft fabrics like chiffons, cottons, voiles, light silks, and linens. Colors are generally lighter as well, and include pretty floral prints for bridesmaids' dresses. Slips made from chiffon cut on the bias are a popular summer look for both brides and bridesmaids. Generally, bridal and bridesmaids' dresses are barer during these seasons. If you are using bare, strappy dresses, it is a good idea to add a wrap in a coordinating style. The wrap will ensure the bride and her attendants are comfortable in an air-conditioned environment, and it allows you to change the look of the bridal party between the ceremony and the reception.

In the fall, the color spectrum includes all the wonderful autumnal shades, such as cognac, brown, earth tones, mustard, and butterscotch. Fabrics for fall are generally a bit heavier than in the spring or summer, and hemlines and sleeves may be longer.

Winter colors tend to be darker shades—even including black for bridesmaids—with jewel tones predominating. Winter fabrics are heavier. The most popular winter wedding fabrics are velvet, four-ply silk, gabardine, wool crepe, and rich brocades that work wonderfully for bodices.

Left: A teardrop bouquet of deep red roses contrasts dramatically against the bride's snow white gown.

SIMPLE IDEAS FOR HEADPIECES

One of my favorite bridal looks, which is very simple, is to have your dressmaker cover a padded headband with the same fabric as the bridal gown and sew a layered veil of diaphanous silk tulle onto the headband. Another idea is to cut an oval of silk tulle about a yard and a half in diameter (unless you want it longer), and sew on a border of a quarter- or half-inch piping of charmeuse silk, then attach the veil with thread to a hair comb. Another option is to cover a hair comb with wedding-dress fabric and adorn it with fresh flowers, or wear a simple, flat "Jackie O" bow of 1 1/4-inch-wide grosgrain ribbon.

HAVING A DRESS MADE

As you look through magazines, you might find you like the skirt of one dress, and the top of another dress. If you know exactly what you want, why not have a dress made to your specifications? Just be sure you can locate the fabric, because most custom dresses are created using a specific fabric. And of course, this approach mandates a skilled dressmaker who knows how to cut a pattern and construct a wedding dress. Always ensure that the dressmaker produces a sample in muslin first, so that the pattern may be adjusted before cutting into expensive fabric.

If you are having a dress made, buy your shoes before you are fitted for the dress, and wear the shoes to all the fittings. You'll break in the shoes a little, and you'll guarantee the proper skirt length.

BRIDAL TRAIN LENGTHS

Bridal dresses are made in a variety of lengths, with and without trains. Some dresses are designed so that the train may be detached for ease of movement once the ceremony is over. Alternatively, your train may be bustled at the back after the ceremony; be sure to check with your bridal salon so that you can do this easily. Trains may be attached at the waist, at the back yoke of the dress ("watteau"), or at the back shoulder ("capelet"). Lengths of trains vary:
• Sweep: falls about six inches on the floor
• Chapel: extends about a foot to eighteen inches on the floor
• Cathedral: extends twenty-two inches or more on the floor
• Royal: extends a yard or more on the floor

WHO PAYS FOR THE BRIDESMAIDS' DRESSES?

It depends on the bride. If she or her family can afford it, paying for the bridesmaids' outfits is a lovely gesture. If that's not possible, the bride might offer to split the cost with the attendants, or the attendants might purchase the shoes while the bride covers the dresses. If the bride is really on a budget, then the bridesmaids would buy their own outfits, and the bride would purchase an accessory, such as a pair of pearl drop earrings or pearl necklace. In such a case, the bride should endeavor to keep the cost of the ensembles as low as possible, and they should definitely be able to be worn again.

Above: This bride wears a romantic Christian Dior gown made of white silk chiffon, with a cummerbund fastened with silk chiffon roses. Below: Bride Erin Malloy wore a powder blue silk shantung gown with a 1950s-style empire waist, three-quarter-length sleeves, and an inverted pleat in the back. Right: An utterly simple A-line dress made of silk crepe is accented with a train bustled in three tiers at the back.

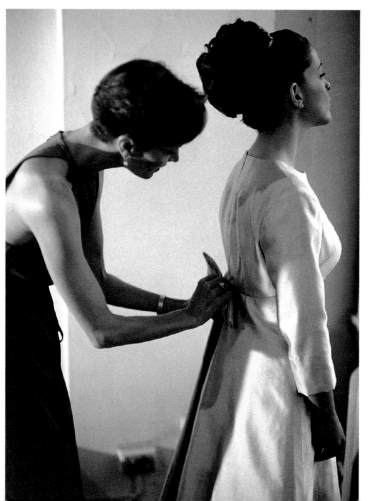

THE COMFORT FACTOR

I advise brides to buy two pairs of the shoes they have selected for their wedding—one in their size and one a half-size larger. Every day for two weeks in advance of the wedding, wear each pair around the house for half an hour to break it in. Bring both pairs to the wedding. You have no idea how often a bride's feet will swell due to stress, hot weather, water retention, or standing too long, and her usual size is painful to wear for an extended period of time. Having the extra pair in a larger size can save the day.

This is also a season where heavy beadwork or decoration with Austrian crystals looks most appropriate. There are no rules regarding sleeve length or cut for winter, but if the dress is bare or strappy, it is a good idea to add a little bolero jacket or luxurious velvet-lined wrap for comfort.

Whatever the season, tulle is the one signature wedding fabric that seems appropriate year-round.

As you think about your dress, the most important factor is the line of the dress and how it works with your body shape. The dress should be comfortable and, at the same time, flatter your body type. If you've got great legs, show them off. If you are long-waisted, avoid a dropped waistline or a dress that cuts you across the middle and emphasizes your torso. If you are full-figured, stay away from flouncy, frilly confections that add bulk to your silhouette. Just because a dress looks good on a size-four store mannequin doesn't mean it will translate to an eight. Try it on, sit down, and move around; don't just stand in front of the mirror.

Comfort and fit are critical. Never buy a wedding dress that is a bit small, thinking you'll diet into it. Spend time and attention on proper fittings—several if necessary—with a professional seamstress. You need a dress that will allow you to hug friends and be comfortable while dining and dancing until dawn, if you want—not something that you have to keep adjusting. If the dress doesn't fit properly, or if it is not comfortable, you are not going to be happy with it on your wedding day.

Proper fit is absolutely crucial for strapless or décolleté gowns. You won't want to spend the entire evening using your elbows trying to keep the dress up because it wasn't constructed correctly. The bodice of strapless dresses must be constructed with bones (stiffeners) that are concealed with multiple layers of China silk, and it should fit like a second skin. Most bridal dresses are heavy and gravity can pull the dress down, which can have a disconcerting effect. If you are wearing a strapless or very low-cut gown, be sure to walk around, bend over, and raise your arms during your fitting so that you can be sure the bodice stays in place.

The right gown will enhance your best features and disguise any figure problems. When choosing a gown, think about the silhouettes and necklines of your most flattering dresses. Consider your best features and how to show them off.

In addition to the silhouette of the dress, it's critical to decide which colors look best with your skin tone. White is not always right for every bride. Few women look really good in true white. Also, it tends to appear bright and flat in videos and photographs. Softer shades of eggshell, cream, ecru, champagne, flesh, or ivory generally are more flattering. Many brides are choosing to be married in becoming shades of soft pinks, peaches, golds, and beautiful autumnal colors like soft brown and even cognac, if these shades work with their coloring. There are no rules. If you look fabulous in celery green and if the dress complements the design of your wedding, then you should be married in celery green!

Top left: A professional dresser, seamstress, or close family friend armed with needle and thread can help the bride get ready and make needed last-minute changes on the day of the wedding. Middle left: Wedding day finery—a crown pendant and South Sea pearl pendant on a pearl necklace, by Cynthia Bach Jewelry Design. Bottom left: A crown bracelet and matching ring inspired by eighteenth-century crown jewels, by Cynthia Bach. Bottom right: Jewels, veils, and dresses do not belong to brides only. Happy in all her glory!

DRESSERS

In most major cities, brides can hire a professional dresser through their bridal salon to assist on the wedding day. The role of the dresser is to make certain that all the bride's attire is perfectly pressed, to arrange all the accessories, and to take care of any last-minute emergencies, such as a ripped hem or loose button. If you do hire a dresser, be sure to discuss what equipment (such as a clothing steamer, safety pins, needle and thread, etc.) she will or will not be bringing.

LESS IS MORE

Regarding personal style, there's an oft-quoted piece of advice that is still true today. As a bride, when you feel you have assembled the entire outfit for your wedding—the dress, veil or headpiece, jewelry, gloves, shoes—put it all on and stand in front of a mirror. Then take off the first accessory or piece of jewelry that catches your eye. That's the element that causes you to look overdressed. You want the ensemble to create an impression of effortless style.

GIFTS FOR BRIDESMAIDS

Silver, gold, or pearl earrings

Pearl necklace or pendant

Engraved silver plate picture frame

Leather travel case for jewelry

Monogrammed fountain pen

Crystal decanter

DEFINING VEIL TYPES

Birdcage is a short, chin-length veil.

Blusher is a sheer veil worn over the face that is lifted during the ceremony.

Chapel extends beyond the gown one to two feet.

Fingertip extends to the bride's fingertips.

Flyaway is a layered, shoulder-length style.

Mantilla is a round veil that is usually made of lace and worn without a headpiece.

Waltz or ballerina length extends to just below the knee.

Cathedral extends two feet or more on the floor. This is a very formal style of veil.

HOW FAR IN ADVANCE TO BUY WEDDING ATTIRE?

Take it from me: the moment you walk into a bridal salon they will tell you they need a deposit right away to ensure you get a wedding dress. I recently visited several bridal shops with a bride whose wedding was more than six months away. We didn't even know where the wedding would be held and all the shops told me they needed an immediate deposit. One bridalwear salesperson told me she needed six months to do the dress. "Forget it!" I said. "You're making a dress, not building a skyscraper!"

Three months prior to the wedding date is the industry standard for ordering a wedding dress. You're probably all right even with two months. And if you haven't selected your dress and the wedding is six weeks away, don't panic. You can still find an appropriate dress and have all the necessary alterations made in time. Naturally, if you are dealing with department store ready-to-wear you'll have much more flexibility.

For men, one month ahead is generally plenty of time to select a suit or tuxedo and have one or two fittings. Custom suiting requires two months or more lead time. If you are renting formalwear, place reservations for tuxedos several weeks to a month in advance of the wedding and go in for fittings immediately so that alterations can be made. Pick up the formalwear several days in advance and try it on one last time with your formal shoes to avoid any last-minute surprises.

THE AMENITY BASKET

All sorts of last-minute emergencies—major and minor—occur at weddings. Headaches, a ripped hem, a torn stocking, hair out of place—you can't anticipate what will happen. The smart thing to do is create an amenity basket that is strategically located in a dressing room or bathroom. Ask an attendant to bring the basket from the dressing area to the ceremony site to the reception locale. The basket should contain the following:

Aspirin or other headache medicine

Bobby pins

Chewing gum, breath mints, and mouthwash

Clear nail polish and instant nail glue

Facial tissues

Hairbrush and comb

Hair spray

Hand lotion or moisturizing cream

Lip balm

Nail file and emery board

Safety pins

Sanitary napkins and tampons

Sewing kit

THE VEIL

Many brides still choose to wear the traditional gown and veil for their wedding. But selecting a veil and headpiece is nearly as challenging as finding the right dress. The key is to look at the effect of the entire outfit: the dress, veil, accessories, and shoes together. The problem is, a lot of brides will buy the dress, then shop separately for the shoes, the veil, and accessories. I advise brides to put on the whole ensemble, stand in front of a full-length mirror, and ask: "Is this how I want to look?" Because while each component on its own might be fabulous, together they might not complement each other and may look overproduced.

When you are considering a veil or headpiece, keep in mind the comfort factor. If you don't want to wear your veil for the reception, make sure it can be easily detached without ruining your hairstyle. Many veils are designed in two pieces: a long veil attached with velcro, worn for the ceremony and then removed, leaving a shorter veil in place for the reception.

Once you have decided on your veil, be sure to rehearse how you will take it off and handle any necessary repair of your hairstyle. If you plan on having your hair professionally styled for the ceremony, take the veil to your stylist for a "dry run" before the wedding date. Too often, brides get pinned, lacquered, and sprayed into their veil to create a perfect effect for the ceremony. When they attempt to remove the veil for the reception, disaster ensues. Of course, many women want to look like a bride for the duration of the festivities, and prefer to retain their veil for the reception.

The traditional veil and headpiece is just one option. Another look is to work with your florist and hairstylist to adorn your hair with fresh flowers, such as stephanotis blossoms, spray roses, and gardenias. If you have long hair, you might simply pin it up with a few fresh flowers. Be sure to schedule an appointment with your stylist well in advance of the wedding to create the style, then take a picture of it as a reference for you and the stylist.

SHOES

The style of your shoe should suit that of your dress. If you are wearing a dress with a full skirt, it tends to call for a more formal, closed shoe. If your dress is very summery, a strappy shoe, perhaps with a higher heel, can be very chic. Of course, it is important to take into account the height of your fiancé.

I feel strongly that bridal shoes should be covered with fabric. White leather pumps are too ordinary for this occasion. Most bridal stores are able to custom-dye fabric-covered bridal shoes to match your dress. These bridal shoes are generally covered with silk file, or ottoman or bengaline, which are finely ribbed fabrics. Alternatively, your shoes can be covered in fabric that matches your dress. Perhaps a small purse can also be covered in the same fabric. If appropriate, the shoes can be adorned with a bow, fresh or silk flowers, rhinestones, or beadwork.

HAIR, MAKEUP, AND PERSONAL CARE

I think it is a wonderful idea for brides and grooms to be pampered on their wedding day. Consider booking a masseur to provide a relaxing massage for you and your groom on the morning of the wedding. You might also schedule a manicure and pedicure. Your bridesmaids would appreciate a professional manicure as they are getting ready as well. These sessions, with all the female members of the bridal party together in a dressing area, can be a lovely time to share with the women you are closest to.

While many brides arrange to have their hair styled and their makeup professionally applied on their wedding day, this is not the occasion for trying out a new face or hairdo. Your wedding day is no time for bold experimentation. As a bride, you should look like yourself at your absolute, natural best.

If you plan to work with a hair or makeup professional on your wedding day, schedule an advance session with each person well before the wedding so that the makeup can be applied and adjusted, and the hairstyle can be refined. If you color your hair, schedule a coloring session as close as possible to your wedding day for maximum color and to avoid dark or gray roots. Try out any unfamiliar makeup line or skin products at least a week in advance to ensure you are not sensitive to them. Always test makeup under the same lighting conditions that will prevail at your wedding. Once you are happy with your look, a snapshot will be a handy reference point on the wedding day.

Also, avoid getting too much sun right before your wedding. It's no fun to be a sunburned bride. Even small amounts of sun can cause facial blotches and may wreak havoc with your carefully planned makeup.

On the wedding day, it works best to apply makeup first and then style the hair. It's easy to touch up your face at the last minute, but more challenging to put life back into a tired hairstyle. A final tip: slip away to powder your nose and reapply lipstick just before the cake cutting—a major photo opportunity.

BRIDESMAIDS' DRESSES

Bridesmaids' dresses have been much maligned over the years—often, deservedly so. Fortunately, a more contemporary approach to dressing bridesmaids has surfaced. Today, a well-designed bridesmaid's dress is just as appropriate at a chic cocktail party as it is at the wedding.

As the bride, the guideline to remember is this: only ask your bridesmaids to wear a dress that you, yourself, would want to wear to a luncheon, cocktail party, or dinner.

Having witnessed countless weddings over the years, I firmly believe that understatement and simplicity are the order of the day for bridesmaids' dresses. Remember that the bridesmaids' role is to complement, not outshine the bride. If the attendants are elaborately dressed, they draw attention away from the bride and groom.

Department stores or boutiques can be a great source for bridesmaid dresses. Visit your favorite store and see what different fashion designers are showing this season. Look at fashion magazines as well as bridal magazines. If you get an idea for a dress that you love but can't find in a shop, purchase some fabric and have dresses made for your attendants. It is no longer necessary for the bridesmaids to all wear the same color, or even the same dress, for that matter. There are four basic approaches to bridesmaids' dresses:

•Identical dresses
•Identically styled dresses in the same fabric, but in different shades of color within the same family
•Different-style dresses in the same fabric and color
•Different-style dresses in different fabrics in an identical shade

For a unified look that still allows for individuality, select a beautiful fabric and have a simple A-line dress made with a slightly different neckline and sleeve treatment for each bridesmaid. This permits each bridesmaid to select the style that is most flattering and comfortable for her.

Another approach is to choose one fabric in a range of colors. For nine bridesmaids in a large wedding, I selected silk dupioni in pale shades of celery, soft peach, lavender, ivory, soft rose, and gray. Each bridesmaid chose the color of dress that was most becoming for her skin type. I had the same fabric pleated and made into matching wraps for each bridesmaid. Before the bridesmaids went down the aisle, we arranged and tied each wrap differently. Some wraps were draped like a shawl; some were swathed snugly off-the-shoulder and tied in front; some were draped asymmetrically over one shoulder and tied at the side. Each bridesmaid had a distinctive look but the whole effect was unified.

I designed a fall wedding in beautiful autumnal colors: cognac, brown, butterscotch, and pumpkin. Since the bride's three bridesmaids all lived in different parts of the country, I went to a fabric store and selected a handful of fabric swatches that matched the color scheme. I cut each swatch into three pieces and mailed them to each bridesmaid with a note asking them to find a dress in any one of the enclosed colors. The result was that the bridesmaids' attire matched the wedding colors perfectly, and each bridesmaid wore a flattering dress that she loved.

Still another option is to pick a color, skirt length, and level of formality and ask each bridesmaid to choose her own dress within those parameters, subject to the bride's approval (out-of-town bridesmaids can send a photograph of the dress). These approaches allow all the bridesmaids to look their best.

Perhaps the simplest idea for bridesmaids' attire is to choose a chic, understated cocktail dress that is available in a range of sizes and flattering to all your attendants. You can always dress it up with a velvet or chiffon wrap, a piece of fine jewelry, a floral bouquet, or other accessories. If you select a becoming dress as your attendants' attire, take it from me: they will be forever grateful and, best of all, they'll wear the outfits proudly.

Think, too, about your bridesmaids' body shapes, and be considerate. Don't dress one bridesmaid; dress them all. Pick a style that will flatter the most difficult-to-flatter bridesmaid. If four of your five attendants are a svelte size eight, but one is a size sixteen, choose a style that is becoming to the larger woman. That way, she won't be embarrassed,

and the other attendants will look great too.

The bridesmaids don't all have to wear the same shoe, but they should all wear the same color and style of footwear, whether a court shoe, a pump, or a chic strappy sandal. It gives the wedding party a more unified, elegant look.

THE GROOM'S ATTIRE

It's so boring to see all the men at weddings standing at the altar dressed like penguins. So many men assume that formalwear is a must for weddings, but it just isn't so. In fact, formalwear for the groom at all but the most elaborate evening weddings is not necessary. Just like the bride's wedding dress, the groom's attire should suit the venue, level of formality, and time of day of the wedding. There is a wide range of menswear possibilities that look handsome on grooms. Be creative.

The groom's attire should complement the bride. A thoughtful fiancé matches his outfit to the style and level of formality of his bride's dress. If she is wearing a plain cream silk gown, the groom's suit should be similarly sleek and understated.

With today's less formal weddings, more and more men are wearing a stylish suit, or even a blazer and a tie, at their weddings. Like the bride, the groom needs to consider his personal taste and what looks good on him. He should think about the colors that complement his skin tones. Some men look terrific in a black suit. For others, the best look is a navy blazer, a crisp white shirt, and pressed khaki trousers with a fabulous tie. Men in the military have the option of wearing their dress uniform, which always looks courtly and regal.

Grooms can even put together an outfit that's stylish and highly personal—a gorgeous pair of fitted tuxedo trousers, a collarless white silk shirt with a decorative button in place of the bow tie, and an ivory shawl-collar double-breasted jacket—elegant and very different. It all depends on the type of celebration and the dress selected by the bride.

Of course, if you are having a formal evening wedding, then you may wish to dress in black tie. But give careful consideration to a black-tie event. The problem with tuxedos is that men who don't own one must rent one. It's hard to find a rented tuxedo that doesn't look like a rented tuxedo. Renting is also expensive.

Even men who do own tuxedos generally don't wear them very often. As a result, men get out their black-tie ensembles at the last minute and realize the pants don't fit. Or the jacket has gone out of fashion. So, think about the style of your wedding before you decide to wear a tuxedo. And I would urge you to think about your guest list before you specify a black-tie affair. You may be asking some guests to spend more money than they are comfortable with.

If you do choose a black-tie wedding, there are many options in formalwear. Leading men's designers are putting more of an edge into their formalwear with new collar designs, decorative buttons, and other touches. A well-fitted dinner jacket can be worn tieless with a wide-collar, open-necked creamy satin shirt. For a more traditional look, consider a plain black four-in-hand tie, or a black satin cravat, instead of a bow tie. Vests are a striking way to tie in with the overall color scheme of the wedding—anything from a rich brocade or pinstripe to hand-painted silk. Vintage ties, cummerbunds, and bow ties are great to incorporate into the groomsmen's formalwear, and make a thoughtful gift from the groom. You can also find a beautiful piece of silk and have bow ties custom-made for the wedding party. Just remember to avoid loud colors and try to keep the look simple and understated.

MEN'S FORMALWEAR TERMS

Black tie: a black dinner jacket and matching trousers, usually worn with a formal dress shirt and bow tie. During the warmer months, a white jacket is sometimes substituted. This look is appropriate for formal evening weddings.

White tie and tails : more formal than black tie, this consists of a black tailcoat with matching trousers, a formal dress shirt with winged collar, a white piqué vest, and white bow tie. This look is appropriate for the most formal evening weddings.

Morning coat (also called a cutaway): a black or gray tailcoat worn with a gray waistcoat and gray striped trousers. This look is appropriate for very formal morning or daytime weddings.

UPDATING YOUR FORMALWEAR

If your groom's tuxedo is looking tired—say, the lapels are too wide, the pants are too tight, or the sleeves are too short—he should go to his tailor and see if it can be restyled. It is often possible to make a few tailoring changes that update the tuxedo completely, avoiding the necessity of buying a new one. Two-button jackets can be changed into three- or four-button jackets. Or sometimes a new shirt together with a pocket square and a pair of great cuff links can transform the outfit.

WHO PAYS FOR THE GROOMSMEN'S ATTIRE?

The assumption (usually correct) is that most groomsmen own a suit or, if the wedding is black tie, a tuxedo. A thoughtful gesture is for the groom to buy his groomsmen a tie, or a shirt and tie. If clothing does have to be rented, the groom can pay for the entire expense or a portion thereof, whatever is most reasonable, taking into account the financial capabilities of all parties.

GIFTS FOR GROOMSMEN

Sterling silver pocketknife

Monogrammed hip flask

Engraved silver plate picture frame

Pair of cuff links

Money clip

Crystal paperweight

Monogrammed fountain pen

Bottle of fine Cognac and two Cognac glasses

If the groomsmen are renting tuxedos, a generous groom might buy each of his groomsmen a fashionable shirt, perhaps one with an interesting collar that doesn't require a tie. This is a very contemporary style that avoids the penguin look.

If you do rent formalwear for your wedding, it's almost never necessary to rent shoes. Rented shoes for men seldom fit right and can be terribly uncomfortable. The groom and his groomsmen only need shoes in the same color; they don't have to be the same shoe. Everyone will look fine and be much more comfortable wearing their own shoes that fit. Just be sure that they are clean and brightly polished.

ATTIRE FOR CHILD ATTENDANTS

If there are children in the wedding party, it can be an opportunity to create the finishing touch. I design the wedding gown first, the bridesmaids' dresses second, the groom and groomsmen's apparel third, then pull the look of the wedding together with the children's attire.

Since the children precede the bride, their outfits should, once again, complement the bridal party and reflect the style and level of formality of the adults' attire. I've done weddings where the flower girl's dress was a miniature version of the bridal gown or bridesmaids' dresses. For an old-fashioned look, the flower girl might wear a dress with a hand-smocked bodice finished with ribbons that complement the color scheme of the wedding. A little girl's dress might be made from remnants of your mother's wedding gown. Another enchanting look is a tulle skirt with spray roses sewn on in little clusters.

There are few sights more charming than a little ring bearer proudly walking up the aisle in a diminutive navy blazer, gray flannel shorts, knee-length white socks, and black shoes. For a formal wedding, the ring bearer might sport a tiny tuxedo. But do keep in mind that very young children can't be expected to wear heavy or elaborate costumes during a long wedding ceremony.

When there will be children in your wedding party, you can encourage them to walk down the aisle by telling them there is a surprise at the end (make sure there is!), and always remind them to smile as they take their walk.

hen people talk about a great wedding they attended, they focus on the visuals—the flowers, the tables, how the room was decorated. Creating a vision of your wedding look and successfully executing it with the use of flowers and other decor elements will personalize your wedding and give it excitement and impact.

While weddings of the past were decorated in shades of white, ivory, and champagne, today the options are limitless when it comes to color and decor. You might be inspired by a favorite film to create your wedding look, like the fourteenth-century wedding scene from *Much Ado About Nothing,* which was rustic and simple, showcasing thick white muslin fabrics and bunches of flowers crudely hand-tied and laid on the bare trestle tables. Or, you might want your guests to feel as if they had stepped into a Tuscan villa, with planters filled with cypress trees, terra-cotta pots overflowing with geraniums, and topiaries made with fresh herbs.

Shaping your vision into a beautiful celebration is challenging, but it should also be exciting and fun. The key is to create the vision first, then think through all the elements so that there is a continuity of style with each element playing off the others. A visually beautiful wedding is one where the decor elements have been planned to work together in a harmonious manner. When guests enter your wedding site, whether it is a backyard or a ballroom, they should immediately sense that this celebration has a unique look that expresses the personality of the bride and groom.

Wedding style has nothing to do with the amount of money you are prepared to spend. I have designed gorgeous weddings that cost a great deal of money, and I have worked with small budgets and created equally memorable celebrations. No matter what the budget, everyone must make choices about how and where to spend money. In the end, none of your guests will know what choices you made. They will only remember the beauty of your wedding and how perfectly the setting seemed to fit the bride and groom.

FLOWERS

Flowers, the "language of love," have figured prominently at weddings for centuries and can help you create a personal style and ambience that will make your wedding unforgettable.

Classic wedding flowers such as lily of the valley, stephanotis, and roses in shades of white, off-white, and pastels used to be the standard approach. Today there are no rules about the color and type of wedding flowers you may use. I have designed many gorgeous weddings that featured brightly hued, dramatic bouquets and table arrangements. At one formal reception I created two completely different and very striking centerpieces. Half the tables featured sumptuous arrangements of deep red, magenta, purple, and yellow roses dripping with bright green amaranthus, and bunches of lightly gilded grapes, cascading from tall silver candelabra that held long ivory candles. On alternate tables stood tall topiaries studded heavily with roses in medium shades of ivory, peach, soft pink, and white. The effect was bold and baroque, and very appropriate for an elegant black-tie party.

Left: A large, opulent-looking centerpiece was created inexpensively by using a faux-finished plaster urn filled with grapes, apples, and vines, studded with occasional rose blossoms and stock.

Some brides are adept at arranging flowers and working with florists. Others can't tell a daffodil from a dahlia. Whatever your familiarity is with flowers, start from square one when deciding what materials to feature at your wedding. Think about the style, theme, and color palette you have chosen, and what type of feeling—formal or informal, rustic or sophisticated—you want your wedding flowers to convey. Look through flower books, wedding books, and bridal magazines for ideas. Clip magazine photos that show floral styles, colors, and arrangements you like—and dislike. Recall the look of a cherished vacation destination or a favorite resort. You might love the formal rose gardens of a historic inn in the mountains, or the creamy white orchids lavishly arranged in the lobby of an island resort in Bali.

The season of the year, and region of the country where your wedding will take place, are also important factors in selecting your floral decorations. Although most good florists can supply almost any type of flower nearly year-round, you do need to make sure that the flowers you select with your florist will still be available for your wedding at a price you can afford.

A referral from a trusted source is the best method of finding a good floral designer. Ask for a recommendation from recently married friends whose sense of style you respect. If you attend an event that had gorgeous flowers, ask who provided them and if the host was happy with their service. Another resource for finding a florist is the catering manager or concierge of a top-quality hotel. It is very important to select a florist who is reliable, punctual, and delivers exactly what was promised, which is why personal referrals are so important.

When you first speak with a florist, check to see if he or she is available on the date you have selected, and make sure the designer will personally install the flowers. Communicate up front your tastes and preferences, and how much money you are prepared to spend. You should ask to see photos of wedding flowers the florist has done and the list of available props. A good florist is able to provide wonderful props for a rental fee that can help you demarcate your space and add atmosphere to your ceremony or reception; the possibilities include balustrades, wrought-iron arches that can be decorated with flowers and greenery, candelabras, pedestals, urns, and battery-operated candles, among many other items.

When selecting the florist to work on your wedding, much depends on the creative interaction that you have with him or her. Even if you are talking with the best designer in town, if there is no rapport between you it may be difficult to get what you want. If you did not have a personal referral to the florist you prefer, obtain a list of references and check them thoroughly.

Once you have retained a floral designer, be sure to provide all the information he or she needs to create the right look. Bring a photo, sketch, or swatch of your wedding dress. Also, bring photos of the ceremony and reception sites to walk your florist through the space. You should also make arrangements for the florist to see your wedding dress and visit your ceremony and reception sites, especially if an extensive installation is planned.

When you and your florist have decided on the whole look of your wedding, which includes linens, china, silverware, and centerpieces, ask

Right: The bride and groom were married next to a beautiful Mediterranean-style fountain, which we filled with rose petals for a romantic effect.

ADVANCE PLANNING

After the date of your wedding is set and you have a concept in mind, for all but the smallest weddings you should hire a floral designer no less than three months before your wedding date. A very popular designer may be booked up to a year in advance. If you are getting married during the busiest wedding season, May through August, you should hire a florist as soon as your date is set. One cautionary note: flowers are more expensive and may be in short supply during peak flower-giving times, such as New Year's Eve, Mother's Day, and Valentine's Day.

When the details of the floral installation have been determined, insist upon a contract that includes all the specifics—the date of your wedding, time of delivery, and a description of the flowers, including a photo of the sample arrangement. Emphasize the delivery times on the wedding day. The flowers for your ceremony and reception should be installed at least one hour before the ceremony begins, and the personal flowers for the bridal party should arrive at least an hour before any formal photos are to be taken. If the temperature is warm, keep the personal flowers in a refrigerator until they are needed. Be very clear about your expectations on timing—it is anxiety-provoking to work with a floral designer who is extremely talented but does not have any concept of time or production. You don't want to have guests walking in the front door as the florist is sweeping out the back door!

the florist to make a sample centerpiece so that you can see it on an appropriately sized table exactly as it will be set for your wedding. You should expect to pay for this, as you would for any floral arrangement. Sometimes a centerpiece that looked fabulous in a sketch or in the florist's shop just does not work on your table when set with all the china and glassware. When doing the sample, have the florist bring extra floral materials so that you can add or subtract until you are completely happy with the color, texture, materials, and design of the arrangement. Be sure to photograph the final centerpiece and give the florist a print of the photo to guarantee that you will get exactly what you were expecting.

CEREMONY FLOWERS

In their colors, types, and style, the flowers at your ceremony site will give guests a hint of what they are to experience visually at the reception. At the ceremony, the idea is to draw attention to the visual focal point where the vows are being taken, and enhance the decor of the site without obstructing guests' views of the bride and groom.

As you select your flowers, be sure they suit the architectural style of the space, whether it is gothic, baroque, country, or contemporary. Sometimes it is not necessary to have extensive flowers at the ceremony; many houses of worship are quite ornate and floral arrangements can get lost in an elaborate setting.

If cost is an issue, I tell clients to spend their money on the flowers for the bride and wedding party—the "personal flowers"—and the area where their guests will be spending the most time, which invariably is the reception. If you are holding your ceremony and your reception at different sites, it may be possible to transport some of the ceremony flowers to the reception area. For example, the flowers that adorned the altar can easily be used to decorate food buffets, or placed at the entrance to the reception. Arrangements that stood at the top and bottom of the aisle may be placed on columns and used at the four corners of the dance floor. Be sure your florist allows for this and is able to move the flowers after the ceremony and install and refresh them at the reception (this can be done unobtrusively during the cocktail hour so your guests will not even be aware of it). Do remember that most churches and synagogues have policies regarding flowers, such as where they may and may not be displayed and when they must be installed and taken away, so it is important to find out what the rules are at your venue.

As you plan floral arrangements at the altar, keep in mind that guests will be viewing the flowers from some distance and possibly from one side only. You need large flowers that have presence, such as big lilies, full-blown roses, hydrangeas, and peonies. The arrangements must be of a certain scale or they will be entirely lost on guests seated at the rear of the ceremony area. Your florist can add height to arrangements by placing them on pedestals or in urns.

Flowers are also often used at the aisles. If you would like to do this, keep in mind the importance of maintaining unobstructed sight lines for the seated guests. Aisles can be accented with nosegays on every pew, or every second or third pew. The end of each pew might have a candelabra, perhaps garlanded with swaths of tulle or chiffon.

Pews may be linked with swags of fabric or lengths of ribbon to keep the aisle clear and the aisle runner clean. Pews can be joined with ropes of tulle or garlands of leaves and blossoms. For one wedding, I lined the aisle with long garlands of smilax, ivy, lemon leaves, and plumosa studded with roses and peonies, which created a lush and natural effect.

At evening ceremonies, candlelight gives a sense of romance and

mystery. Candles can be arranged on simple or ornate candelabra around the altar and placed in tall candleholders at the ends of pews. Another approach is to cluster hundreds of votive candles en masse, which creates an extraordinarily romantic, warm effect. However, many ceremony sites prohibit the use of candles. If your site does not permit candles, your florist may be able to rent battery-operated electric flickering candles with decorative lamp shades that can be covered in fabric to complement your decor. The electric candles look very realistic and create a romantic ambience without the danger of fire.

An aisle runner is a long piece of fabric or carpet that runs the length of the aisle, creating a special walkway for the bridal procession. In the olden days, when every bride wore a long train, the aisle runner kept it from getting soiled. Now, the runner is used to heighten the drama of the bride's entrance.

Fabric runners may be rented through your florist. While disposable paper runners are available, I prefer the look of a fabric runner, and a rented fabric runner is also more environmentally friendly because it is reused many times. Pure white linen or white satin acetate both make lovely aisle runners. Placing a pair of floral arrangements on each side of the runner where it meets the steps leading to the altar gives the effect of flowers bursting out of the pathway. One way to add drama to the bridal procession is to keep the aisle runner rolled up at the altar until just before the bride makes her entrance, then have two ushers roll it out slowly down the aisle.

If you are being wed outdoors or in a space that does not have a demarcated aisle, you have the ultimate freedom to define the space any way you wish. The bridal path might weave through the guests in an S curve demarcated by rose petals. Or, the bride might circle around all the guests and walk to the center of the circle, to be married in the round.

For a home wedding, indoors or out, use flowers and greenery to create a focal point where you will be taking your vows. Outdoors, a floral arch or a trellis may be used to showcase the bride, groom, and officiant. The easiest and least expensive way to create a floral arch is to find a pair of tall, slender flowering trees or shrubs in pots, and join their tops. You can enhance the arch by fastening additional blossoms, floral moss, and ivy to the branches. Florists can also fabricate beautiful arches. A steel frame may be covered with dried or fresh honeysuckle, grapevines, and lots of ivy; then bricks of floral oasis wrapped in chicken wire may be attached and studded with your favorite flowers.

Indoors, creating a focal point for your ceremony can be as simple as placing your largest candelabra on the mantelpiece and draping it with leafy garlands studded with flowers and fruits. Or have your florist create a gorgeous arrangement that cascades down one side of the fireplace. Another approach is to use a pair of standing arrangements, such as flowering trees or topiaries in urns, or arrangements cascading down from atop a pair of pedestals. During the fall, include groupings of fruits, such as red apples, pears, and pomegranates, accented and pulled together with lightly gilded leaves and clusters of candles. An even simpler look is to flank the bridal party with a pair of dramatic standing candelabra that hold a brace of flickering candles. The candelabra may be rented from an antique or housewares shop.

Left: A gazebo was created by placing trellising over an arbor framework and covering it with roses, ivy, vines, and bunches of grapes. The floor was carpeted with pieces of inexpensive sisal matting stitched together.

PERSONAL FLOWERS

THE BRIDAL BOUQUET

The bride's bouquet is an accessory, just like her headpiece, shoes, and jewelry. It should be scaled to the bride's size and shape, and designed to complement her wedding dress and color scheme. For bridal bouquets, big is not necessarily better. It takes a tall girl to carry a large bouquet gracefully.

Bridal bouquets can be wired, which means that every flower is individually wired into place; or hand-tied, which means the flowers are gathered with a ribbon and tied together. Hand-tied bouquets are usually less expensive and look less formal. Long-stemmed flowers, such as delphiniums, long-stemmed roses, calla lilies, and French tulips, work particularly well in hand-tied bouquets.

What's possible with bridal bouquets? The answer is anything. For a petite bride, picture a small pomander, shaped like a heart and composed of dozens of tiny pink rosebuds, hanging on a gold silk rope from her wrist. Since the calla lily has long been considered a classic art deco motif, what could be more dramatic for a bride wearing a sleek art deco–style gown than an armful of calla lilies lightly dusted with gold powder and tied with white satin ribbon? At an autumn wedding, themed around rich fall colors, the bride might carry a tight bouquet of ivory roses with a collar of deep brown Leonidas roses. For an early spring wedding, consider a bunch of daffodils tied with a ribbon.

For a dramatic but very simple bouquet, have a skilled florist fashion one large "flower" using many blossoms. When dozens of individual gladiolus blossoms are glued together into a camellia bloom, it is called a glamellia. It is also possible to use dozens of individual rose petals to construct a stunning oversized rose bloom twelve or fourteen inches in diameter.

Fabric from the bride's or bridesmaids' dresses can also be made into fabric flowers that are interspersed with real blooms. For a winter wedding where the bridesmaids wear the same style gown in different jewel-tone shades, remnants from each dress may be used to fashion brightly hued fabric roses that are interspersed with the fresh flowers. For a vintage look, antique glass-beaded fabric roses can be wired into a floral bouquet.

Just like a finely made garment, the way a bridal bouquet is finished off shows its quality. The bouquet should always be carefully taped and finished with ribbon so that it looks elegant even when you place it down.

If you prefer not to, you don't have to carry a bouquet. Some alternatives you may want to consider include a boa made of vibrantly colored blooms such as peonies, roses, and astilbe, or a thin garland of miniature roses hand-stitched to the neckline of your dress. Flowers may also be pinned in your hair or wired to a comb used in an upswept hairstyle. Freesia, gardenias, roses, gypsophila (by itself only), and stephanotis work particularly well in hairstyles.

If you are thinking about carrying a single flower because of its simplicity, remember a single flower does not look half as good as it would if surrounded by others of its kind.

If you do carry a bouquet, for photographs be sure to hold the bouquet low, below your navel. Holding the bouquet low makes you look taller and slimmer. A short-waisted bride can elongate her look by carrying a trailing, pear-shaped bouquet.

Overleaf, left: Brightly colored roses are tied tightly together with viburnum blossoms. Overleaf, right, top to bottom: Porcelana roses studded with blossoms of stephanotis and wrapped in silk tulle; daffodils; viburnum with a cuff of scented geranium leaves.

TYPES OF BRIDAL BOUQUETS

Wired bouquet: a bouquet where the stems are individually wired into shape

Teardrop: a tight cascade bouquet in the shape of a teardrop

Nosegay: an upright bouquet

Cascade: a bouquet that falls forward in a cascade

Arm bouquet: a bouquet that is loosely held on one arm

Pomander: a tightly constructed bouquet in a three-dimensional shape, such as a globe or heart, that is completely covered in blossoms. Pomanders are usually carried on a rope or ribbon.

Hand-tied bouquet: a bouquet of flowers that are not wired but fastened together with ribbon

Left: A variety of hand-tied nosegays. Top to bottom: Tulips with bear grass; Virginia roses; Message roses with stephanotis blossoms tied with a cuff of camellia leaves; stephanotis. Above: Freesia tied with a cuff of rose leaves. Right: Keep all personal flowers refrigerated until the last minute to prevent them from opening prematurely.

Below: Seashells were used to personalize this bouquet for a bride who was getting married at the beach. Right: Hand-tied nosegays. Top to bottom: Porcelana roses cuffed with Leonidas roses and camellia leaves; sorbet-colored roses; Sensation roses with cattleya orchids and stephanotis blossoms.

Overleaf, left: Nosegays of different-colored roses were created for each bridesmaid. Overleaf, right, top: Bridesmaids' bouquets of green hydrangeas, bluebird roses, and cuffs of scented geranium leaves and a bride's bouquet of lily of the valley with a cuff of scented geranium leaves. Overleaf, right, bottom: An arm arrangement of white roses, hybrid delphinium, and lizyanthus.

By ordering a separate tossing bouquet from your florist, you can preserve your bridal bouquet as a keepsake. The tossing bouquet is usually fashioned along the same lines as the bridal bouquet but is smaller, lighter, and less expensive. During the reception, the tossing bouquet is traditionally placed on the cake table.

Your bridal bouquet can be professionally preserved by your florist, or you can dry the bouquet yourself. Air-drying the bouquet is easiest. Simply remove the foliage; retie the bouquet with cotton string and hang it upside down in a dry area where it will not be disturbed. The process usually takes several weeks. Or, you may use a dessicant, such as silica gel or borax. Get instructions from your florist in advance of your wedding. If you intend to preserve your bouquet, plan ahead so that it can be done as soon as possible after your wedding. During the reception, have your mother or a friend mist the bouquet lightly and refrigerate it in order to keep it fresh.

ATTENDANTS' BOUQUETS

Once the bridal bouquet has been designed, the flowers for the rest of the wedding party can be chosen. The bridesmaids' flowers should complement the bridal bouquet, either in color, texture, shape, or materials, but on a smaller scale. For instance, if viburnum is one of the flowers used in the bride's bouquet, then all the bridesmaids might carry nosegays of viburnum on its own.

One of my favorite things to do is to create completely round nosegays for the bride and her attendants. A lovely style is the French nosegay, composed of roses in different colors that are arranged in concentric rings. A light cloud of tulle may be wrapped around the bouquets, studded occasionally with a stephanotis blossom held in place with a pearl pin. At a wedding that takes place at the beach, perhaps streamers from the bridesmaids' bouquets could have tiny shells attached.

The maid or matron of honor may carry a bouquet that is slightly different from those of the other attendants.

Flower girls look adorable wearing headbands or head wreaths decorated with blossoms, or carrying pomanders or floral wreaths. With little girls, the key is comfort. Be sure their headbands or head wreaths don't pinch and aren't too heavy.

Traditionally, the mother and grandmother of the bride wore corsages. Today, many women prefer to carry a small nosegay or spray of flowers during the ceremony.

Always keep photography in mind when designing the personal flowers, advises floral designer Walter Hubert of Silver Birches, in Los Angeles. Photography accentuates contrasting colors, and causes similar shades to blend into each other. If the attendants' dresses are aubergine, and the bouquets are aubergine with a few white flowers, the camera will pick up only the white flowers. The silhouette of the bouquet should contrast with the garment so that the flowers will show up in photos.

GROOM'S AND GROOMSMEN'S FLOWERS

Just as important as the bouquets for the bride and bridesmaids, are the boutonnieres of the groom, groomsmen, and other men in the wedding party. The groom's boutonniere is not necessarily larger, but more distinctive than the others because of its color or the type of flower selected.

Top left: A classic French nosegay using different flowers in concentric circles. Bottom left: A summery hand-tied bouquet of white lilac and lavender sweet peas.

A tasteful, masculine look may be created with a boutonniere that consists of one or a few small blooms—tight rosebuds, stephanotis blooms, a single gardenia blossom, two blooms of freesia, or several of lily of the valley. The boutonniere can be enhanced with a bit of greenery, like a camellia or lemon leaf, or a sprig of eucalyptus or lavender. A sprig of holly is a handsome touch for the greenery during the holidays. The boutonnieres are usually attached with a sturdy pin to the left lapel of the jacket.

If your wedding is a large one, I suggest ordering a second boutonniere for the groom. By the time the groom gets to the cake cutting (a big photo opportunity) he has hugged and kissed at least a hundred people, and that boutonniere will look like it has been run over by a two-ton truck! With a fresh boutonniere, the groom will look his best all evening.

RECEPTION FLOWERS

As in the theater, what happens during the first five minutes sets the tone for the rest of the evening. First impressions are extremely important. Consider how to accent the entrance to your reception to give it a welcoming feel that will draw the guests inside. One approach is to drape the doorway with leafy, blossom-studded garlands or simple swags of tulle. Other ideas are to flank each side of the entrance with a rose- or fruit-studded topiary on a pedestal; adorn a pair of tall standing candelabra with ivy and flowers, or use tall floral arrangements from the ceremony site. If you are to be married under a floral archway, perhaps the archway can be moved from the ceremony area to the rece tion site to create a dramatic entrance. Always be sure that the entryway is properly lit to increase the visual impact of your floral arrangements.

Create the feeling of a gracious entry hall by placing a round table with a huge arrangement of flowers near the entryway. This is also a good spot to put place cards, or the guest book.

Once your guests are seated at tables, the centerpieces will be a focal point. Don't skimp on the centerpieces, and make sure they are lit properly.

Centerpieces can range from a cluster of tiny clay flowerpots brimming with posies and interspersed with votive candles, to lush arrangements of dozens and dozens of blooms. Your first consideration is to make sure seated guests can see across the centerpieces directly into the eyes of the person opposite them. A visual barrier between guests at the table hinders conversation and dampens the energy of the group. Centerpieces should either be low—no higher than fourteen inches—or high and narrow, so as not to block sight lines.

Centerpieces should fit the overall look and color scheme of the wedding. There is no rule that says you must have only one type of arrangement, or that all the floral vessels have to be identical. Why not visit flea markets and collect vintage serving pieces to use as floral vessels for your tables? Another option for a country-style outdoor reception is to fill old glass milk bottles with assorted field flowers. You can also use groups of three or four tiny glass vases abundantly packed with flowers and surrounded with votive candles. And you're not limited to flowers; ornamental kale and sprigs of rosemary, lavender, and thyme work beautifully in centerpieces. Fresh fruits, such as tangerines or kumquats on leafy branches, apples, grape bunches, and pomegranates are easy to work with and provide great visual impact for less money than flowers.

For a more formal wedding, you can alternate between tall candelabra adorned with cascading bouquets of flowers, and low, tightly packed, dome-shaped arrangements. Both centerpieces are very elegant, and the contrast gives visual interest to the room.

For a crisp, contemporary look, use massive quantities of gypsophila on its own in a centerpiece on white tablecloths. It creates a lovely cloudlike effect. These centerpieces may also be alternated with tall candelabra surrounded by gypsophila at the base.

Another approach for a clean, minimalist look is to use only white flowers and fabrics, and bright green leaves as color accents. A dramatic aisle runner may be created with thousands of bright green galax leaves glued to a length of fabric. Fashion a chuppah by gluing galax leaves to completely cover four poles, and stretching white spandex overhead.

Calla lilies, long-stemmed creamy white tulips, white orchids, and bear grass all work extremely well in sleek, modern floral designs. Or roll up curly willow and place it inside a bubble vase, then use it to arrange your flower stems. You can also spray the curly willow gold or silver first.

Alternating gilded urns with gilded candelabra, and using trailing amaranthus, abundantly arranged flowers in bold colors, and lightly gilded pomegranates or grape bunches creates a rich, baroque effect.

I often use quite a bit of ivy and other trailing greens like amaranthus and smilax in centerpieces. The trailing greens create a relationship between the centerpiece and the tabletop, which gives it a harmonious, natural look.

One type and color of flower used en masse in all the arrangements creates a strong visual impact that is contemporary and very impressive. Flowers that work well en masse include hydrangeas (in the same shade or a multitude of shades), roses, peonies, sweet peas, and tulips.

I usually design two different centerpieces for the tables at large weddings. One centerpiece is tall and one is low, and they are placed on alternating tables throughout the room. This approach breaks up the space, and it avoids that convention-hall look that one sometimes sees at large events.

For an informal wedding reception, such as a breakfast or Sunday brunch, I love to use baskets lined with moss and abundantly filled with fresh strawberries, creamy stephanotis, and ivy trailing onto the table. Another pretty look is to plant small wooden boxes with flowering bulbs, such as hyacinths or daffodils. For a charming woodland effect you can plant a basket with small flowers like violets, and add moss, herbs, baby mushrooms, and a few quail eggs.

Buffets are the place where you can use dramatic materials such as flowering tree branches and tall, large flowers such as peonies, big lilies, and full-blown roses. The large size of buffet tables requires arrangements that are larger in scale for greater visual impact. I often like to elevate the flowers on a buffet table to give them more stature and presence.

In designing your buffet arrangements, it is important that your florist coordinates closely with your caterer or hotel food and beverage manager to determine how the buffet table will be laid out and to ensure that there is adequate space for the food and the flowers.

Right: Virginia, Timeless, and Daniella roses tightly packed with lily of the valley in a silver punch bowl.

Overleaf, left: A glass cylinder filled with oranges and kumquats gives an autumnal look to this dramatic buffet arrangement. Top right: A cascade of multicolored roses surrounds tapered candles in this tall candelabra arrangement, which preserves sight lines across the table. Middle right: A topiary of lemons and moss stands in a clay pot finished with a variety of mosses. Bottom right: A formal rose topiary is arranged in a faux painted "antique" pot.

Preceding spread: A formal wedding in a tent featured the lavish use of brilliantly colored flowers. Centerpieces were tall candelabra cascading with vibrantly colored roses, cattleya orchids, and smilax. Tables covered with gold organza skirting were arranged around a checkered dance floor that was enclosed with a balustrade and accented with topiaries.

Above left: Strawberries, lily of the valley, stephanotis blossoms, and ivy are arranged in a moss-lined wire basket. Above: A simple arrangement of white spray roses in a glass bubble vase that has been covered with moss and studded with seashells and dried starfish. Right: A water pitcher and a sugar bowl become floral containers, filled (respectively) with white peonies and white roses.

Left: For a fall wedding on a tented tennis court, the ceiling was abundantly swagged with mint-colored chiffon and hung with chandeliers for soft ambient lighting. The flowers, in autumn colors, included roses and amaranthus combined with lightly gilded grapes and pomegranates. Below: A richly patterned floral damask completed the look.

USING FLOWERS AND PROPS

When you walk into a typical banquet hall or hotel ballroom for the first time, it is often difficult to imagine how you can transform a boxy, plain space with bad lighting, low ceilings, and sometimes no windows into a beautiful setting that reflects your personal style. One of the most effective ways of doing this is with decor elements and props that generate a feeling of warmth and a welcoming ambience.

Flowers, decor elements, and lighting may be used throughout the reception area to create warmth and intimacy and highlight focal points, such as the dance floor, the bridal table, the wedding cake, and the band. Vertical elements, such as columns, trellises, and potted palms or trees help break up the room so that it doesn't look like a sea of tables.

To highlight the bridal table at a dinner, you might surround it with four columns draped with garlands of flowers. Or, use a different centerpiece on the bridal table, as we did at one wedding where the bride and groom sat at a table accented with a family heirloom crystal candelabra.

Your florist can rent a variety of architectural elements, props, and other items to enhance your decor, including plants and trees—potted topiaries, palm or ficus trees, and low hedges. To create a country garden look, border the dance floor with a row of Eugenia hedging in white garden boxes. For a Mediterranean look, trees may be adorned with lemons, limes, or kumquats. Or, mimic the look of topiary by using architectural elements, such as obelisks or cones, thickly covered with blossoms or studded with fresh fruits. At night, twinkle lights in trees give a dazzling effect. If the ceilings in the room are high enough, a great way to set off the dance floor is to place tall trees or columns on the four corners of the dance floor, and up-light the trees using lights placed inconspicuously on the floor. Choose leafy palms for a casual effect, topiary for a more formal style, and cypress for a Mediterranean look.

Below left: Flowers and greens adorn a fountain, tiebacks, and a chandelier. Below middle: A blanket of wheat grass covered the floor of a vintage birdcage that was used as a prop for a garden wedding. Below right: Tieback garlands are composed of roses, peonies, and greens. Right: An antique wire chair, found at a flea market, was decorated with wheat grass, a posy of roses, a cuff of peonies, and table smilax, then used as an accent at the entrance to the reception tent for a garden wedding.

MY FAVORITE BRIDAL BOUQUETS

Most of my favorit e bridal bouquets are very simple.

• A hand-tied bunch of lily of the valley, wich is so delicate looking and has a wonderful fragrance.

• A nosegay of stephanotis blossoms, because stephanotis is such a sculptural, waxy-looking flower and when packed tightly together it makes a gorgeous bouquet.

• A hand-tied bouquet of fragile sweet pea blooms in different pastel shades, because of its simplicity.

• A tight nosegay of roses in an assortment of sorbet colos—raspberry, mango, lemon, and lavender. The softness of the colors is enchanting.

• A nosegay of daffodil blooms with their stems wrapped in silk ribbon or adorned with silk rope and tassels.

BRIDESMAIDS' BOUQUETS

A few ideas for bridesmaids:

•An exact replica of the bride's bouquet, but in a smaller size.

•Bouquets of roses, a different color for each bridesmaid.

•Each bridesmaid carries a bouquet composed of a different type of flower, but matched to the same color, such as cream or soft pink.

•For bridesmaids wearing the same style dress but in different hues, tie their bouquets with ribbons that match their dress color.

•Select a single flower that was used in the bride's bouquet and use it en masse for the bridesmaids.

•For a country wedding, bridesmaids can carry arm bouquets of field flowers tied with organza ribbons.

•If the bridesmaids' dresses are lavender, have the bride carry a lavender bouquet and the bridesmaids ivory or white bouquets. Obviously, this works with other colors as well!

PERSONALIZING YOUR TABLES

A lovely way to make guests feel welcome is to have each guest's name written in calligraphy and set in a tiny picture frame at each place setting. The frames may be engraved with the bride and groom's names and the date of the wedding. After the wedding, send guests a small print of a wedding photo to place in the frame as a keepsake.

In many of the parties I do, I try to create a residential feeling that personalizes the space. You can use furniture, such as sofas, chairs, and various types of tables, to demarcate spaces in the room. Accessorize the pieces with lamps, framed paintings, decorative pillows, and flowers. Antique shops will often rent furniture for special events, and the right antique sideboard or crystal chandelier can create the feeling of being entertained in an elegant home. If you are using a hotel space, sometimes the management can be persuaded to let you use furniture from other areas to enhance your space.

I often rent one or more working fountains to create a focal point for a garden reception. A large fountain might be placed at the center of the space, or wall-hung fountains can be placed around the perimeter. The fountains can be decorated with wreaths of gardenias or other flowers, and beautiful fully blown blooms may be floated in the water.

Columns or pedestals are another great prop that adds an architectural element and allows you to demarcate spaces and create drama. Your floral designer or wedding consultant can work with you to locate the right decor elements to enhance the theme of your wedding reception. When arranging to rent props, be sure that they will be delivered in plenty of time and installed correctly. Coordinate everything with your florist so you don't have to learn how to wire a fountain at the last minute.

Sometimes rental or hotel spaces have unattractive ceilings. These can be concealed while creating a softly tented look by draping swags of fire-retardant tulle, chiffon, or other suitable fabric from the central point in the ceiling down to where the ceiling meets the walls. The fabric ceiling can also be washed in colored lights. If the ceiling is low, draping it will only accentuate the low height. Instead, place columns around the room and use lighting to draw the attention to your tables and away from the ceiling.

LIGHTING

The saying "It's all about lighting" is 100 percent true. The most beautiful flowers, tablecloths, and decorations are to no avail if the space for your ceremony or reception is badly illuminated. If your ceremony and reception are to be held during daylight hours, lighting is less of a concern. For an evening reception or during the transition time between dusk and night, use lighting to create a warm ambience. Spotlight objects you want guests to see. At night, anything you do not light will disappear. Imagine spending months designing the look of your wedding, down to your colors, flowers, room decor, and wedding cake, and because of inadequate lighting the subtlety and beauty of your decoration are lost.

Proper lighting is so important that I always advise clients on a budget that if they had planned to spend a certain amount on centerpieces, they should cut back by 25 percent and use the savings to hire a lighting company. You can spend hundreds of dollars on a centerpiece, but if it is not properly lit at night, your guests won't be able to see it.

Be sure you see your space under the same lighting conditions as will be present at the time of your reception. Think about how to highlight the buffets, the dance floor, the band, the tables, and the cake. The goal is to create a softly lit evironment that is flattering to your guests and conducive to having a good time.

Preceding page, top: Sheer fabric is used to create another dimension in the ceiling of a tent. Middle: Abundant drapings of white cotton fabric, bathed in amber light, create a dramatic effect over a dance floor. Bottom: A pair of drapes, simply tied back, gives drama to this canopy entrance.

FLORAL COLORS

In discussing floral colors with florists, I find it helpful to refer to different families of color.

• Full color includes primary and secondary colors in strong, vivid hues such as red, blue, bright pink, magenta, purple, green, and bright yellow.

• Medium colors are less intense shades, including soft pink, lavender, peach, ocher, butterscotch, and moonlight (light yellow).

• Soft colors are very light, pale tones such as ivory, mushroom, white, and creamy yellow.

Be aware of these color families as you select your flowers. Mixing these color families can give a three-dimensional effect to your arrangements, as the contrast makes the colors of the individual flowers stand out. An arrangement of creamy roses will look even more beautiful with contrasting bright white roses.

GET IN EARLY

Wherever your ceremony is being held, find out how early that day you can gain access to the space so that you and your vendors can properly prepare for the wedding. Complex floral, lighting, and sound installations require considerable time. If you are using live music, additional time must be allowed for musicians to rehearse and tune up. Often, churches book back-to-back weddings, and have other services planned, which may make it a challenge to set up for your ceremony.

This becomes even more important if you are holding your reception in a rental space or hotel. When you first contact the hotel, it is absolutely critical that you find out what time you have possession of the room. Ask if you have the room for the full day, or even the evening before. Often there may be other functions booked in that same space for earlier in the day, which means your florist won't be able to install your flowers until late. It may be possible to pay extra to secure the room from nine A.M. on, or from whenever you feel you need the space.

At the other end, if you anticipate your party will go late, find out if there is a time by which you have to be out of the room, and see if that is negotiable. Many times the room is booked on a Sunday after a Saturday event, and a premium may be charged to pick up after your party.

SERVING PIECES

Note that if you are mixing your own or borrowed serving pieces or decor items with those of the rental company, caterer, or florist, take an inventory of your pieces and go over the list with each vendor. Point out each piece and explain how it will be used. Write down the name of the person who will be responsible for returning the items to you and ask your wedding coordinator or a friend to check them off the inventory as they are returned at the end of the evening.

IDENTIFYING THE PERSONAL FLOWERS

Give the floral designer a list of everyone in the wedding party who is to receive personal flowers. The florist should then identify each bouquet, corsage, and boutonniere with a name tag to ensure that everyone who is supposed to receive flowers gets the proper piece. Remember that you don't want to be bothered with these details while you are getting ready for your big day.

BILLETS-DOUX

It is a lovely idea for the bride to hand-write a short note to her groom and give it to the florist to place with the groom's boutonniere. If she likes, she can also add a little gift to dress up his wedding attire, like a pair of vintage cuff links or an antique watch. So much of the preparations on the wedding day focus on the bride. It is very moving to watch a groom take out his boutonniere, read the note from his bride, and realize she is thinking of him at that particular moment.

Left, top to bottom: Lighting is one of the most important elements of an evening wedding because it highlights what you want people to see while darkness hides what you want to disappear.

IDEAS FOR AISLE TREATMENTS

Crisp white linen runner

White satin acetate runner

Fabric runner covered with galax or lemon leaves

Thick carpet of rose petals

Thick carpet of dried leaves

Try to create a balance between ambient lighting, which lights up the entire room, and spotlighting, or pin spots, which are focused beams of light. Keep the ambient house lights very low and use candles and pin spots to focus light on just those elements you want the eye to see. This romantic lighting style creates a wonderful mood in the evening. To achieve this, all house lights must be on dimmers. If they are not, it is easy and inexpensive to have dimmers installed. If that is not possible, here is a tactic that doesn't cost a penny: ask for light bulbs to be unscrewed (but left in the sockets) until the light level is as low as you wish.

For the ceremony, you want lighting that highlights the area where you will take your vows, whether before an altar or in front of an ample fireplace. A candlelit ceremony is charming and romantic in the evening, although for photographs you will probably want enhanced lighting at the focal point. Front-lighting is not the only option. At one wedding that took place outdoors at dusk under a rustic floral arch, we backlit the arch in amber, which bathed the bride and groom in a warm, flattering glow as they took their vows.

For the reception, the lighting should be as low and as intimate as possible, with spotlighting or pin spots used to highlight focal points in the room. Use pin spots to light centerpieces, buffets, the wedding cake, and decor items. Softer diffused lighting is focused on the dance floor and the band. Avoid fluorescent lighting at all cost; this harsh, unflattering light kills a party.

Colored lights can be used to achieve specific effects. Gels (clear colored plastic inserts) may be added to existing light fixtures. Or, a specialty lighting company can provide colored light bulbs. I recommend using soft pink and light flesh-tone gels wherever people or food need to be lit. Soft ambers and light gold also complement skin tones. Blues and greens tend to make people look unattractive. Green works very well to light trees and foliage, and blue should be used to light water.

Gobos are metal disks with a cutout pattern through which spotlights may be shined to project a pattern or message on a flat surface, such as a ceiling or wall. There are stock gobos in standard cutout shapes, and custom gobos, which are ordered to project a personal message or a custom design. A mottled pattern gobo, projected down onto the tabletops, gives a layered, textured look to the lighting. This effect can also be used to light a dance floor.

Sometimes specialty lighting companies can go overboard. Too much lighting can give an event an overproduced look. Remember, lighting fixtures are not attractive and should be concealed as much as possible with plantings or fabric.

If you are hiring a lighting company and planning a large installation, ask for a standby lighting specialist to be in attendance to make any necessary adjustments and handle problems, such as refocusing lights if tables have been moved, or moving a light that is shining in a guest's eyes.

If specialty lighting is not in your budget, you can still create a warm ambience with candles. A wonderful romantic effect can be created with a low centerpiece surrounded with lots of candles. Table lamps with low-wattage bulbs and fabric shades make for a romantic, intimate feeling.

Right: A shower of rose petals is a fun ending to a ceremony. They can be presented in a variety of ways, such as a cone formed of antique music sheets (or photocopied music sheets), a cone of handmade paper with the name of the bride and groom and the date of the wedding written in calligraphy, or even simple rustic buckets garnished with roses and ivy.

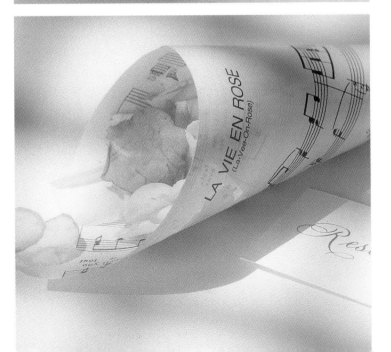

SAVING MONEY ON CENTERPIECES

There are many ways to create beautiful centerpieces on a budget.

•Keeping in mind that a large vase takes a huge amount of cut flowers, use instead three to four small vases, packed tightly with full-blown blooms. This gives the impression of abundance while using relatively few flowers. Intersperse the vases with three or four candles in mismatched glass or silver candleholders, or little votive candles.

•Look for interesting floral containers at offbeat sources: wholesale floral markets, stores in ethnic neighborhoods, mail-order catalogs, flea markets, garage sales, and local mass merchants. Start collecting well in advance so you have plenty of time to select the best pieces at the lowest prices.

•If it fits your theme, use gorgeous fresh fruit in your centerpieces—clusters of grapes, bright oranges, apples, and pomegranates, which gives a lovely Italianate effect. The fruit takes up space, allowing you to use fewer flowers.

•Use just a few large, expensive, full-blown roses in each arrangement to create a lavish look.

•For an outdoor country-themed wedding, fill twelve- or fourteen-inch low terra-cotta planters with soil and moss and plant violets, paper whites, daffodils, hyacinths, pansies, mixed ranunculus, or other favorite flowers and herbs. These make great party favors for guests at the end of the evening.

TECHNIQUES

•To give a burnished look to soft fruits such as grapes, use a light dusting of gold or silver powder or spray paint. For hard fruits such as pomegranates, applied gold or silver leaf works well.

•To make sugared fruit for centerpieces, separate an egg and paint the fruit with the egg white using a brush. Then roll the fruit in crystalline or extra-fine sugar and let it dry. Grapes and small fruits such as peaches, plums, and long-stemmed strawberries work best with this treatment.

•To age terra-cotta pots, sponge them lightly with varying shades of green and off-white paint. Then dab them lightly and unevenly with glue and roll them lightly in floral moss. Let them dry overnight. New clay planters will look like they have been in a potting shed for ten years.

•Inexpensive plaster containers may be given a patina of age by spray-painting them gold, then using a sponge to add mottled shades of brown and olive green.

Create an organic look for your floral containers by spreading them thinly with glue or using a hot-glue gun, and applying a thick coating of floral moss. Alternatively, glue galax or lemon leaves all over each container by using spray adhesive on the leaves and applying them to the container one at a time.

CHAIRS

If the chairs at the location you have selected are not what you had in mind, you have a couple of options. You can rent chairs from a local rental company, or you can cover the chairs. This is done by wrapping the chair backs or the entire chair in fabric, or by renting slipcovers. Slipcovers come in a variety of colors and fabrics, ranging from plain white, ecru, and pink cotton to expensive-looking damasks and romantic sheer chiffons.

If you wish to rent chairs and are planning a formal wedding, the best-looking and most comfortable chair is called the Ballroom, Charivari, or Whitehouse chair. These are usually available in gold, silver, fruitwood, mahogany, natural, or white. Most rental houses have a variety of seat cushions that can be coordinated to your decor. A less expensive alternative is a white or natural wood folding chair. If you can't find the chairs you want, try renting them from a local hotel.

Keep in mind that it may be possible to use the same chairs for the ceremony as for the reception. During the cocktail hour, the waiters or valet parkers can move the chairs from the ceremony to the reception area. Slipcovers may be placed over the chairs to give the reception seating an entirely new look.

LINENS

Gone are the days when weddings meant white hotel-style linen cloths. Today, damasks, stone-washed florals, moire taffetas, ginghams, satins, and fine vintage or new linens, in every color of the rainbow, are all possibilities for weddings. There are several specialty linen houses that deal extensively in mail-order linen rental and will ship your linens directly via common carrier. Your florist, wedding planner, or banquet manager can recommend and provide the names of national linen rental companies. Be sure to arrange a delivery date that is several days in advance of your wedding.

With linens, you may use one cloth per table, or layer different-sized cloths for varying effects. To give an antique look to your wedding, tablecloths can be made from inexpensive calico cotton or muslin, sized extra large, so that the fabric puddles on the ground. Soak the cloths in a bathtub filled with tea to turn them an antique ecru color. Then, overlay each table with a lace cloth for a charming effect. Another option for a more casual look is to stonewash floral-patterned upholstery fabric until it has an irregularly faded look.

It is not necessary for all the tablecloths to be the same color. Another option is to choose cloths in the same fabric but with several different colors that harmonize with each other.

Shimmery, iridescent organzas can be used as table overlays or even chair covers for a gala, dressy effect. Just as you save shimmery dress fabrics for gala nighttime affairs, these types of fabric are really only appropriate for evening weddings, when they can be very dramatic if done tastefully. You can pair a shimmery organza with an underlay in the same or a contrasting color.

Even if you are using a hotel's linens and napkins, you can personalize the look by swagging masses of tulle or muslin around the tables. Every few feet, the tulle is gathered with wire and fastened to the underskirt with thread; then the gather may be decorated with a few fresh blooms.

THE RING BEARER'S PILLOW

If you are using a ring bearer in your wedding, your florist can make the ring pillow more beautiful with a variety of floral materials. Be sure to fasten the rings onto the pillow with a half bow of ribbon so that there is no danger of the rings being lost during the ceremony. Here are some suggestions for enhancing the presentation of the rings:

• Upholster a ten-by-ten-inch cushion with extra wedding dress or bridesmaid's dress fabric; adorn it with fringe, tassels, or braid and attach a few fresh flowers.

• Cover the top of the pillow with floral moss and stud it with fragrant gardenia blossoms or clusters of small spray roses.

• To make floral "tassels" for the ring pillow, thread a stack of four stephanotis blossoms on strings with beads tied to the end and attach the tassels to the four corners of the pillow.

• Cover a small box with glued-on leaves, rosebuds, or faux pearls and place a tiny satin pillow inside to hold the rings.

BRIDE AND GROOM CHAIRS

The chairs of the bridal table, or just those of the bride and groom, can be enhanced by decorations.

•Garland the chair backs with the same flowers used in the centerpieces, adding accents of tulle and ribbon trailing down the sides.

•Wind a leafy garland studded with a few fresh lemons, limes, or kumquats across the chair backs.

•Cover the chairs in slipcovers or a fabric that matches the tablecloths.

•Attach handsome tassels in your color palette to the chair backs.

•Wrap the chairs in soft chiffon and attach small floral nosegays to the chair backs.

•If slipcovers are too costly, obtain a few yards of fabric, wrap it around each chair back, and tie it with a bow, like a scarf.

BATHROOMS

A thoughtful host pays special attention to the bathrooms at the reception facility. These facilities often have fluorescent lighting, which is terribly unflattering. If your guests are the only ones using the bathrooms, you might consider turning off the fluorescent lighting and adding your own floor lamps. Incandescent lighting can be improved by replacing harsh white bulbs with pink ones or adding a dimmer.

You can also dress up the bathrooms with personal touches that will make your guests more comfortable. Put out your favorite soaps, hand towels, potpourri, fragrance spray, or scented candles. In the ladies' room, add an amenity basket with hair spray, hairpins, a comb, brush, mints, mouthwash, aspirin, tampons, sanitary napkins, facial tissue, and a needle and thread. In the men's room, fill a basket with aspirin, mouthwash, a comb, mints, and facial tissue.

If you are holding a large reception, it is a good idea to hire an attendant to staff the bathroom. The uniformed attendant should have cleaning supplies available. Women's and men's rooms should have appropriate toiletries. The attendant should make sure the room looks just as immaculate by the end of the party as it does at the beginning.

Times have changed, and so has the way we regard weddings. There are more interracial and intercultural marriages than ever before. Brides may be a little older; grooms are more involved in the celebration; the couple may be paying for their own wedding—people want to do things differently. There are no rules anymore.

Despite all these changes, everyone who plans a wedding, large or small, wants to have a fabulous party. You want to create that magical moment when you look around the room and each element is working in harmony—the flowers on the tables look gorgeous, the band sounds wonderful, the energy is high, the dance floor is full, and the air is filled with music and laughter.

Creating a great party may at first seem challenging, but it actually can be fun. You will learn there's a simple formula to entertaining. Start with the basics—delicious food, a good bar, great music—and build from there!

THE REHEARSAL DINNER

The rehearsal dinner is a great opportunity to kick off a wedding celebration. Since this event typically involves many fewer guests than the wedding, you have the flexibility to do something casual and different. It doesn't have to be a dinner. It could be a luncheon, a barbecue, or even a festive Friday evening happy hour.

Although the rehearsal event need only involve those in the wedding party, it is thoughtful to invite special friends who have traveled to the wedding from out of town. In such a case, ask other local guests to provide transportation to the out-of-towners. Guests who are not members of the wedding party should not attend the rehearsal; they can proceed directly to the party.

The rehearsal dinner should be fun and upbeat, and in no way upstage what will happen the following day. Floral centerpieces are a lovely touch, but keep the decor understated. As you plan the rehearsal dinner menu, avoid serving any of the principal dishes that will be featured at the wedding. If you assign seating with place cards, you can balance the energy of the room, encourage guests to make new acquaintances, and avoid the embarrassing situations that can arise when family members who don't get along are seated near each other.

Above all, create an ambience that is conducive to lots of toasts, speeches, and well-wishing. And make it an early night so everyone can get enough sleep before the wedding day.

PLANNING YOUR RECEPTION MENU

No matter what your circumstances—a small budget, a limited choice of caterers, religious food restrictions—it is possible to have a well-designed menu and serve delicious food at your reception. Great food doesn't require a large budget, but it does require forethought, planning, and common sense.

First, take a realistic look at your budget. You should never have to skimp on the quality of the food and beverages served at your reception. It is better to scale back on the limousines and the designer wedding dress. If you spend your money on your guests, you'll have a great wedding!

Start conceptualizing the menu well before you meet with your food-service provider, whether it be a caterer, hotel food and beverage director,

or restaurant. First, consider your personal food likes and dislikes and those of your fiancé. Create a "wish list" of the foods you both love and a list of definite dislikes, just as you did in planning the theme for your wedding.

For inspiration, think of your favorite dishes and the kinds of restaurants that you most enjoy. Would you like to feature traditional or ethnic fare at your reception? Are there foods that your religion prohibits you from serving? How formal or informal will your reception be? Consider your guests—is it a meat-and-potatoes crowd, or a group of friends who enjoy gourmet cuisine?

If you adore down-home Southern cooking, why not serve a great buffet of Southern specialties, like fried chicken, black-eyed peas, corn bread, deep-fried catfish, and hush puppies? Does your groom love stone crab? Indulge him with fresh stone crab flown in from Florida for the reception.

Does the location of your reception suggest a theme for the food? A reception at a yacht club would suggest delicious local seafood, perhaps even a clambake. A home wedding might have an American country theme to the menu.

Consider any limitations of your venue or chef. An outdoor site without access to a food-service kitchen means that most of the food must be prepared in advance and finished on-site. A leading hotel chef should be able to produce an excellent quality menu, while a catering firm working in a home has many of the same limitations as an outdoor site, in that much of the food will have to be prepared in advance in an institutional kitchen. Ask to see sample menus and study them to get a feeling for the chef's specialties. Then, work with the chef to design a menu together that suits the chef's capabilities and experience and fits your taste. This approach will help ensure the best quality food for your reception.

Another consideration is the time of year. Winter is not the season for cold poached fish, nor is an outdoor wedding in July the occasion for prime rib. Heartier fare, such as hot soups, stews, roast beef or lamb, and potato dishes, works better in the winter. Lighter foods, such as fish, salads, and fresh vegetables, come to the fore during summer's heat. While people enjoy light fare during the summer, they usually don't want the entire menu to be light. A deliciously light summer menu can end delightfully with a decadently rich dessert.

Although many weddings are followed by a dinner reception, you shouldn't feel locked into a full sit-down dinner. Consider an early morning wedding breakfast, a hearty winter luncheon, an elegant afternoon tea, or a chic cocktail party. It is better to hold a simple event that you can carry off graciously than to overextend your resources and have to skimp. Pick a few elements and execute them superbly rather than trying to accomplish something beyond your means.

Once you have decided on the basic concept for your reception, it's time for you to select a caterer or chef. If you need to find a catering company, there are several ways to obtain reliable leads. The best florists and party rental companies in town generally know the best caterers, because they often work side by side. The food and beverage director of a good hotel should also be able to recommend skilled caterers that work outside the hotel. Another source is a friend who entertains frequently and whose style you respect. Of course, if you attend a catered event with delicious food, be sure to get the name of the caterer. Always check with the host or hostess to make sure they would use that firm again. The food may be delicious, but the process of working with the caterer should be enjoyable as well.

Meet with several catering companies to discuss your reception. A good caterer or food and beverage manager will be able to take your ideas and preferences and use them to design a menu that is just right for your wedding. Be aware of how responsive the caterer is to your ideas and how well you get along. If you don't have a rapport with the caterer at the first meeting, he or she may not be the right choice. Work carefully with the chef and schedule at least one advance tasting to be sure the food will meet your expectations.

It's a good idea to ask for written proposals with budgets from at least two catering companies. This way you can compare the ability of each caterer to respond creatively to your food ideas, and also get a firmer handle on the range of costs.

Many people think that a favorite restaurant is the ideal choice to cater a wedding. In some instances that may be true. But preparing food in a restaurant is different from cooking on-site at a party, where a hundred portions or more of each course may be needed simultaneously. A good caterer understands how to prepare and serve large quantities of food without sacrificing quality. If you would like to have a restaurant cater your reception, check references to ensure that they have experience with catering large events successfully.

STYLES OF SERVICE

The first decision with a reception meal is whether it will be buffet-style, sit-down, or a combination of the two. Buffet-style is a more casual way to serve a large group of guests. Sit-down is considered more elegant and may be costlier. Depending upon the style of your wedding and the menu design, a combination of sit-down and buffet-style can work well. If you decide to serve a buffet, serving the first course at table can help minimize lines at the buffet for the main course. As plates for the first course are cleared table by table, it creates a natural staggering of the times that guests visit the buffet for their main course.

Try to avoid the look of a hotel Sunday brunch. Those "groaning board" buffets with dozens of dishes may look lavish, but you're not doing your guests any favors. It is better to select one main course and just a few side dishes to make a delicious meal. If you do want to serve several entrée choices, such as chicken, beef, and fish, be sure to place them at different buffet tables with the appropriate accompaniments. This will ensure that guests dine on a well-thought-out menu. Using smaller plates encourages guests to visit each station individually and means they will enjoy the dishes in appropriate combinations, as they were planned. Smaller buffets also allow guests to pass more quickly through the buffet line.

If you like, you may serve a multicourse dinner buffet-style. This is done by either featuring the different courses at different buffet stations, or by changing the buffets while guests are eating each course. Again, it is important to design the buffet so that the foods complement each other.

While buffets should not feature dozens of dishes, they should be filled with plenty of food. There's nothing more forlorn than a long buffet with three dishes on it. Keep your buffets smaller and be sure the food is arranged and presented abundantly.

DEVELOPING THE MENU

In creating a menu, start in the middle, with the main course, to determine the ingredients and ensure they are not repeated in the other courses. For large dinners, try to keep the main course simple. It's much better to dine on a delicious, moist chicken breast than on some

MENU TIPS

Ingredients in a menu should be varied from course to course. A mushroom in puff pastry appetizer should not be followed by a main course of steak in a mushroom sauce. Instead, choose a different sauce, such as a Bordelaise.

Consider contrasting textures and crunch. Garlic mashed potatoes, purée of peas, and steamed whitefish all have a similar soft texture. Instead, choose textures that contrast, and add crunch for flavor interest, like a crunchy coating on the whitefish, or a side dish of vibrant, crisp-tender snow peas.

For beautiful presentation, always be sure your food has contrasting colors. For example, a dinner of roast lamb, a lentil stew, and assorted mushrooms may be delicious but is visually uninviting. Substitute fresh green vegetables for the lentils, and add a dish that contrasts in color and texture, such as carrot flan. Sprigs of vibrant green Italian parsley or another fresh herb can add visual interest, aroma, and flavor to a plate. As you plan the look of the plate, it helps to draw sketches of the foods using colored pens.

It is also a good idea to alternate hot and cold courses, unless you are holding a summertime celebration and are serving an entirely cold meal.

A menu with too much last-minute cooking can cause problems. Make sure your menu is designed so that most of the preparation can take place in advance.

For receptions at home using the kitchen oven, check that the oven is working properly, temperatures are calibrated correctly, and the chef's pans will fit inside.

A TIP ON TIPPING

If you want to ensure that you receive special attention, advance remuneration can work wonders. The day before a wedding I give the chef, the maître d', the head waiter, and any other top service staffers an envelope containing a personal note and a significant cash tip. The amount to tip depends on the service expected from them; the chef should receive the largest tip. Remember, the time to do this is *before* the wedding. These professionals may be involved with a number of events similar to yours. A cash gratuity in advance helps raise your reception to an extra-special level for the people who can make a difference.

MENUS

Having a printed menu at each guest's place setting is a gracious touch that guests appreciate. Menus can be hand-lettered in calligraphy for an elegant effect or can be inexpensively done in script on a home computer. Carefully hand-tearing the edge of the paper using a ruler can give a handmade look to printed menus. Menus can be placed at every place setting, or two on a table in silver picture frames, or on the buffet tables.

SERVING THE FOOD

Never place a first course on the tables when guests are not yet seated. Food deteriorates; people don't! Serve the first course once your guests have taken their seats and begun talking among themselves. Bring the food out to an audience. It's much more elegant.

SOMMELIERS

If fine wine is a focus of your reception, one option is to hire a sommelier, or wine steward, to supervise the wine service. A sommelier adds a level of professionalism to the wine service, and will ensure that wines are poured in the correct order and into the appropriate glasses. A good sommelier can also advise you on wine selection. Most hotels or wine retailers can recommend a sommelier who may be available to work at your reception.

"fancy" overcooked meat in soggy puff pastry. Once you have decided on the main course, you can add side dishes, first and second courses—or however many you desire—appetizers and an incredible dessert to finish the meal.

The golden rule is to balance the menu with a variety of foods that have different flavors, textures, colors, and temperatures.

THE COCKTAIL HOUR

At wedding receptions, the cocktail hour traditionally provides a transition between the ceremony and the meal. It allows time for guests to move from the ceremony to the reception. Often, it provides time for formal photographs of the wedding party to be taken.

Today, many bridal couples are less interested in formal portrait photographs and prefer the photographer to capture more candid pictures. Other couples choose to have formal photos taken before the wedding. These approaches reduce the time needed for photography and allow the bride and groom to enjoy part of the cocktail reception with their guests.

The cocktail hour should whet guests' appetites for the meal they are about to savor with a few carefully chosen, tasty appetizers and good beverages. This is not a time for a constant stream of heavy, filling hors d'oeuvres. Avoid buffets at a cocktail reception, except when serving a type of appetizer where the actual service is a focal point, such as an oyster bar where oysters are being shucked to order, a caviar bar with its accompaniments of crème fraîche and minced onion, or a smoked salmon station where a waiter is slicing the salmon.

For most cocktail hours, I advise serving two to five types of appetizers, and limiting the time to forty-five minutes to one hour maximum. As with the rest of the menu, the cocktail party appetizers should be balanced to vary taste, texture, temperature, and color, and planned so as not to repeat ingredients that will be featured in the dinner to come.

THE FIRST COURSE

Food is like theater. As with a good play, what happens during the first five minutes sets the stage for what is to come. It is vital that the first course at your reception be spectacular in terms of its presentation and flavor.

Think about the visual impression your first course will make, and work with your chef to design the plate. In addition to its appearance, the first course should taste delicious and have elements of color, texture, and temperature. It also has to be able to hold in the kitchen in case you and your groom are delayed with the photographer or at the cocktail party. Examples of good first courses that can be served at table or buffet-style are:

•a rustic soup, like a minestrone with colorful cut vegetables, served in individual bread *boules* (small hollowed-out bread loaves), because it may be kept warm on the stove until just before time to ladle it out

•antipasto plate, because it offers a variety of tastes, textures, and colors and will hold well at room temperature

•composed salad, tossed with dressing at the last minute so that the lettuce doesn't wilt, served on a large dinner plate and topped with grilled shrimp or sautéed scallops and crispy leeks

•chilled vegetable terrine with baby lettuce leaves, which is a colorful dish that really combines two courses (first course and salad) in one

•puff pastry box filled with asparagus tips and tomato, which makes an elegant three-dimensional presentation for a formal dinner and can be

GLASSWARE AND WINE SERVICE

Frequently, you will find that the wineglasses available at a hotel, or from a caterer or rental company, are too small. To properly appreciate its bouquet, wine demands a large glass that is only partially filled. Pick the largest glasses that are available (sometimes a "water" glass is best) and specify that the servers are to fill glasses to an agreed-upon level. A four-to five-ounce pour is a good size for a glass of wine. Request that waiters,guests ask if they would like more wine before refilling glasses.

For champagne and sparkling wine, the flute glass, with its long, narrow shape, is best. The saucer-shaped champagne coupe tends to spill easily and causes the bubbles to dissipate too quickly.

One hint if you are serving champagne or sparkling wine to a large number of guests: trays of glasses can be partially pre-poured up to ten minutes in advance, then topped off with fresh bubbly right before serving.

APPETIZING ADVICE

Creative presentation can enhance tray-passed appetizers. Always make sure the trays are dressed to look more attractive—with a doily, greens, or flowers, depending on the style of your party. Any flat surface can become an eye-catching tray.

•Use serving pieces that you've found at estate sales; they don't all have to match.

•Use bamboo dim sum steamers lined with flat green leaves.

•Fill flat trays with rinsed dried white or black beans or clean polished black stones, then place the appetizers on top.

•Use a piece of slate.

•Press leaves between two sheets of glass and arrange the appetizers on the glass.

•Limit the number of appetizers on each tray so that they stay neat. Instead of thirty appetizers, place fifteen on the trays and have the waiters refill them more frequently.

•Serve only one kind of appetizer on each tray. It looks better; it's easier for guests to decide whether or not to take one; and it's easier for the waiters to remember who's been served which appetizer.

•Be sure the appetizers can be eaten in one bite. It's more elegant and less messy for guests who may be juggling a cocktail and purse.

•Skewered appetizers are popular but problematic—what to do with the skewer when the guest has eaten the appetizer? Make sure the waiters stay near after serving guests to accept used skewers. Guests can poke used skewers into a half lemon, apple, or cantaloupe turned upside down on a tray.

•If you are serving caviar of exceptional quality, have waiters pass a silver tray with the caviar tin showcased in the center, surrounded with a circle of mother of pearl or demitasse spoons filled with individual portions of the caviar.

assembled at the last minute to keep the puff pastry crisp

•a duo of chilled summer soups, such as roasted red and yellow bell pepper soups, or a pale pink and a fuchsia borscht, poured *carefully* and simultaneously into the bowl and garnished with crème fraiche and finely minced chives

•a large dinner plate entirely covered with a paper-thin layer of sliced smoked salmon, with a dollop of crème fraîche, a spoonful of caviar, and warm toasted brioche folded in a dinner napkin at the side.

Another option for a first course is to have waiters bring an assortment of hors d'oeuvres to the table for guests to share. A basket of fresh breads along with a platter of oven-roasted red peppers, stuffed zucchini, prosciutto rolled on grissini (breadsticks), marinated Roman-style artichokes, and grilled vegetables, along with olive tapenade and extra-virgin olive oil for the breads, works well. For a seaside wedding, another delicious first course that can be shared among guests at the table is a platter of chilled seafood, including shrimp, Alaskan king crab, oysters on the half shell, and wonderful cocktail sauces.

THE INTERMEZZO

The intermezzo (in-between) is a sorbet course that is served to cleanse the palate before the main course of a formal, multicourse dinner. Generally, an intermezzo would not be served at a dinner of less than four courses. However, during the summer months it is a lovely idea to serve a sorbet as a meal opener. A tomato sorbet with a splash of frozen vodka and a fresh basil leaf is a great summertime starter.

THE MAIN COURSE

The main course is the centerpiece of the meal. Begin by designing the main course and then add complementary appetizers, other courses, and desserts.

Some caterers and hotels recommend offering a choice of main courses at wedding dinners. This approach is expensive, however, because extra meals must be prepared in order to accommodate all the guests. Another way to accommodate your guests is to have the caterer or hotel prepare a certain percentage of alternate meals that can be provided if a guest does not wish to take the main selection and requests something different.

Keep in mind that hot food must be served hot, and cold food must be served cold. If you are working in a situation where an institutional kitchen is not available, such as an outdoor location, and you are considering a hot main course, ask the caterer if the plates can be heated. A cold plate will quickly absorb the heat from hot foods. If the plates can't be heated, it is a good idea to avoid serving hot courses.

Keeping cold dishes cold is equally important. Inadequate refrigeration can lead to a food-safety problem.

BEVERAGES

One of the key ingredients of a great party is a well-chosen beverage selection. Nowhere in the book of rules does it say that you have to serve champagne at your wedding. It's fun to take a creative approach to your beverages. Why not have waiters pass trays of cocktails, such as Manhattans, martinis, or vodka gimlets? Serving champagne cocktails is another idea that is festive and can be done with an inexpensive domestic sparkling wine. Always be sure to have an assortment of nonalcoholic beverages for your guests as well.

The selection of modestly priced but well-made wines from all around the world has never been better. Keep an open mind. The right selection for your party might be a sparkling wine from the Loire, a robust shiraz from Australia, a merlot from Chile, or a pinotage from South Africa.

If you are holding your reception at a hotel, look over the wine list after your menu has been determined. The hotel should be able to offer several selections in your price range. If you are working with a caterer or doing the reception on your own, the easiest method for selecting the right wines is to fax your menu to the most popular wine shop in town and ask them to make several recommendations in your price range. However, there is no substitute for tasting the wine yourself (which can turn into a fun occasion!). Purchase a bottle of each wine you are considering and taste them with your reception menu before you make the final decision.

When buying wine, beer, and spirits through a retailer, ask whether you can purchase on a consignment basis and return unopened bottles for a full refund (note that some state liquor laws may prohibit this). Keep in mind that if the labels are damaged, the bottles may not be accepted for return. Instruct the bar staff to slip bottles into plastic bags before they are put into ice buckets, to protect the labels. Also, tell your caterer and bar manager that bottles are not to be pre-opened en masse but opened just before they are needed.

Wedding receptions are almost synonymous with champagne or sparkling wine. Champagne is a term that actually applies to wines only from France's Champagne region east of Paris. If your budget will permit it, French champagne is the ultimate sparkling wine for a reception. There are many nonvintage brut (dry) champagnes that offer great quality and are fairly reasonable in price.

California and the Pacific Northwest produce a range of excellent sparkling wines that are made using the same methods and grapes as are used in France's Champagne region. Look for the term *méthode champenoise* on the label to be sure you are getting a top-quality sparkler. These bubblies are generally far less costly than French champagne.

If you are on a tight budget, remember that inexpensive sparkling wine can be enhanced with a splash of *crème de cassis* (blackcurrant liqueur) to make a kir royale, or a spoonful of peach or raspberry coulis. Mimosas (sparkling wine and orange juice) or bellinis (sparkling wine and peach juice) are festive for daytime receptions and don't require an expensive bottle. Bellinis, kir royales, or raspberry kir royales also make a delightful accompaniment to dessert and cake.

For tasting fun, pair an ingredient or dish with its classic beverage match. Guests enjoy the opportunity to try the two together, and it makes for great eating and conversation.

Smoked salmon	Frozen vodka
Gravlax (cured salmon)	Frozen aquavit (a colorless spirit flavored with caraway seed that is popular in Scandinavian countries)
Caviar	Champagne or frozen vodka
Stilton cheese	Port
Foie gras (goose liver)	Sauternes (a sweet white wine from France's Bordeaux region)
Wedding cake	Demi-sec (slightly sweet) champagne

Classic cocktails are back. In addition to a full bar, it is fun to offer one or two classic cocktails, such as Manhattans, martinis, or old-fashioneds, that are pre-poured, placed on silver trays, and offered to guests immediately after the ceremony. To lend a Southern flair, serve mint juleps in glasses that have been kept in the freezer until frosty. For

LARGE-FORMAT BOTTLES

Large-format bottles of sparkling wine, such as magnums, double magnums, or even Methuselahs, make a reception even more festive and create a focal point out of the beverage service. Bottles are available in a range of sizes:

Bottle		750 ml
Magnum	2 bottles	1.5 liters
Double magnum		
or jeroboam	4 bottles	3 liters
Rehoboam	6 bottles	4.5 liters
Methuselah	8 bottles	6 liters
Salmanazar	12 bottles	9 liters
Balthazar	16 bottles	12 liters
Nebuchadnezzar	20 bottles	15 liters

a Southwestern touch, serve an on-the-rocks margarita. Guests enjoy trying something other than their "usual" white wine, champagne, or sparkling mineral water.

Nothing caps off a festive evening more than a sip of Cognac and the aroma of a fine cigar. A novel way to serve an assortment of after-dinner drinks is to rent a vintage serving trolley from an antique store, and stock it with a selection of Cognac, Armagnac, single-malt Scotch, and a liqueur or two, as well as a humidor, cigar cutter, and matches. A bartender can wheel the cart from table to table and present the selection to guests. If a drinks trolley isn't possible, have the waiters circulate among the guests with silver trays holding glasses of pre-poured Cognac and liqueurs. It adds another element of energy and excitement that keeps the party moving.

Another option is to set up a station offering after-dinner drinks and cigars. You may wish to designate a cigar-smoking area, such as a patio, balcony, or small area set off from other guests, so as not to annoy nonsmokers.

THE ADVANCE TASTING

After you have determined the menu for your reception, it is always a good idea to schedule an advance tasting with the hotel, caterer, or restaurant. The tasting is designed to let the client see the presentation of the food and taste the dishes as they will be served at the event. The client has an opportunity to comment and suggest changes, if necessary. The tasting should only be done when you have retained a caterer and your menu has been determined. Ideally, it should be scheduled close to the time of your wedding so that your suggestions and changes will be fresh in the chef's mind. The tasting is the best insurance you can have that your reception will feature great food and that there will be no surprises. The tasting also provides an opportunity not only to see how the food looks on your plates, but to see your tables as they will be set and decorated for your reception, if you make arrangements in advance with your florist.

While you may bring several people with you to the tasting, don't expect the chef to prepare a complete meal for each; it's a tasting, not a meal. The chef will prepare one or perhaps two servings to show how they will be presented at your event, and then the servings may be divided among the group so that all can taste.

Bringing a gift to the chef at the tasting can work wonders. A bottle of fine champagne, or a *cru classé* Bordeaux from a good year, with a handwritten note, shows more than appreciation. It makes a statement about your own sense of style.

Please be sensitive to the feelings of the chef. Professional chefs have had lengthy training and work experience. Some chefs may not take criticism well. As when making any kind of criticism, offer positive observations first, then couch your comments as suggestions. Use phrases such as "could you possibly" and "do you think this looks a bit . . ." Leave the chef room to offer alternatives.

It is perfectly appropriate to make suggestions regarding presentation, saucing, flavor, how the vegetables are cut, the quantity of food on the plate, and so on. But don't wait until the tasting to say that you dislike or are allergic to a food.

If extensive changes need to be made, sometimes a second, or even a third tasting is necessary to refine the dishes and get everything right. Be diplomatic and encouraging so that the chef will feel motivated to create exactly the sort of meal you envision. Document verbal comments with a cordial fax or note.

A fabulous wedding reception doesn't have to be a six-hour extravaganza that includes cocktails, dinner, and dancing. There are good reasons to consider alternative receptions. A low-key celebration with friends and relatives is appropriate if it is not your first marriage. Maybe you and your fiancé are paying for the reception yourselves, and need to stick to a budget. Perhaps you aren't comfortable at large parties and would feel better about a gathering of just fifteen to twenty close friends.

There's no reason to hold a large dinner reception if that doesn't suit you. What about an afternoon wedding followed by an elegant tea party? Or a Saturday morning civil ceremony, followed by a sumptuous wedding breakfast? A late-afternoon or early-evening wedding and cocktail party reception is still another approach that allows you to entertain any size group with style.

A WEDDING BREAKFAST

The wedding breakfast has a long history, although it's somewhat of a misnomer. Traditionally, a wedding breakfast was actually a luncheon following a morning ceremony. It is very festive to update the tradition by serving a sumptuous breakfast reception after a morning wedding. A sit-down breakfast is a bit more elegant than a brunch, usually served buffet-style after eleven A.M.

Wedding breakfasts are a great idea for a bride and groom who want something low-key but elegant. One advantage of this approach is that it is far easier to find a location for a breakfast than it is for a dinner reception on a Saturday evening in June. Breakfast also works well during spring and summer, when you can serve outdoors in the garden under a canopy or market umbrellas.

The setting may be anywhere from a backyard garden to a private dining room at an elegant hotel. Pick a weekend morning and invite guests to witness the ceremony at nine-thirty or ten A.M. Engage a harpist to provide soft background music. Perhaps you start with coffee and croissants upon guests' arrival before the ceremony. After the ceremony, waiters can pass trays of tangerine mimosas (sparkling wine and tangerine juice) or fruit juices.

The menu is colorful, very elegant, and light yet satisfying. Start with a first course of a compote of seasonal fresh fruits, such as figs, prunes, and apples. For the main course, a paper-thin slice of smoked salmon is laid on toasted brioche, then topped with a poached egg and garnished with a few spears of steamed and peeled fresh asparagus to add a bit of green to the plate. A velvety mousseline sauce (a hollandaise lightened with whipped cream) studded with a few caviar eggs adds delicate flavor. While good caviar is expensive, you can use it sparingly and still feel luxurious. The wedding cake is filled with a luscious mixture of fresh peaches with sweetened whipped cream.

What could be simpler? And the bride and groom have all afternoon to start their honeymoon trip.

Compote of Fresh Figs, Prunes, and Apples

Poached Eggs and Smoked Salmon on Thick Toasted Brioche
with Asparagus Spears and a Caviar Mousseline Sauce

Vanilla Wedding Cake with
Peaches and Whipped Cream Filling

Sparkling water
Blood Orange Mimosas
Coffee

A SUMMER LUNCHEON

A luncheon is a wonderful approach to a wedding reception, because it is much less involved than a dinner yet still is an elegant way to entertain. For a wedding luncheon, invite guests to witness a noon ceremony, then serve lunch by one P.M.

This summer luncheon menu begins with a first course of chilled soup, then continues with a main course salad that is strikingly colorful and tasty. The salad of greens, vegetables, and grilled salmon is topped with thinly sliced leeks that have been deep-fried until golden brown and crispy, and a "confetti" of diced mango and red and yellow bell peppers. Each plate looks like a celebration! A trio of intensely flavored home-made fruit sorbets accompanies slices of lemon-flavored wedding cake.

Incidentally, one of the virtues of this particular menu is that it does not require an elaborate kitchen setup to prepare, and all the courses may be done ahead, with the exception of the salmon, which is grilled at the last minute.

Chilled Tomato and Lobster Bisque with Crab

Grilled Salmon on a Salad of Assorted Greens,
Asparagus Tips, Artichoke Hearts, and Baby Potatoes
Topped with Crispy Leeks and a
Confetti of Mango and Red and Yellow Bell Peppers

Trio of Sorbets:
Mango, Passion Fruit, and Litchi Sorbet
with Long-Stemmed Strawberries

Lemon Wedding Cake

Alsace Riesling
Sparkling water
Coffee

A WINTER LUNCHEON

This luncheon menu features hearty winter flavors yet is astonishingly light. It begins with an attention-getting tomato and beet "cappuccino," a little glass eggcup filled with a warm tomato and beet purée, with a bit of cream poured in slowly over the back of a spoon to create a white layer—hence the name. A piquant salad is enriched with bits of roasted tomato and a spoonful of goat cheese mousse.

The entrée is a succulent filet of John Dory, pan-seared and served with braised endive and lentils scented with truffle jus.

For dessert, a classic vanilla wedding cake with a rich vanilla butter cream is updated with a filling of exotic fresh figs.

Tomato and Beet "Cappuccino"

Salad of Mâche with Roasted Tomato
and Goat Cheese Mousse

Pan-Seared John Dory with Braised Endive and
Lentils with Truffle Jus

Dense Vanilla Wedding Cake with
Fresh Fig Filling and
Vanilla Butter Cream Frosting

Dry California Chenin Blanc
Oregon Pinot Gris
Coffee

AN AFTERNOON TEA

Afternoon tea has an atmosphere of age-old elegance that is all its own. You can offer the most exquisite food to guests—dainty finger sandwiches, tiny canapés, light scones, delicate pastries—at relatively little cost. If you serve an afternoon tea buffet-style, you can entertain several dozen guests with just a couple of servers and a bartender.

Afternoon tea is served at three P.M. and is usually a very elegant affair. High tea is a much heartier meal and is served at five-thirty or six P.M.

An afternoon tea reception is a great occasion to use vintage linens and lacy tablecloths. Layer the cloths on buffet tables for a lavish, old-fashioned look. During warm weather, consider borrowing or renting large market umbrellas to shade the food and the guests. Drape the umbrellas with crocheted lace tablecloths or lacy fabric. Borrow or rent extra chairs and cocktail rounds (small thirty-six-inch round tables) for seating.

Serving pieces should be elegant, although they needn't match. You can rent a silver samovar for the tea and silver trays at a local rental company, or borrow pieces from friends or the local hotel or country club. Serve buffet-style, with tea sandwiches and savories on one buffet, desserts and wedding cake on another, and the tea in between.

Recordings of quiet jazz, or classical English baroque pieces played on period instruments, suit the setting. For live music, a strolling violin combo or a harpist and flautist might play soft background music as guests are mingling.

An afternoon tea may be catered, but since most of the food is prepared in advance, such a party is well within the capabilities of home cooks.

The beauty of afternoon tea is it can range from buffet service to a full formal served tea. It can take place in the garden during the summer or be served by the fire in winter, and be equally charming.

Start with champagne or chilled iced tea during the summer, or a glass of sherry in the winter, and continue with hot tea service. This afternoon tea menu features classic finger sandwiches such as cucumber, egg salad, and deviled ham with tomato, served in a bread *boule*, a round hollowed-out loaf.

The secret to dainty finger sandwiches is thinly sliced bread, which can be flattened with a rolling pin. The smoked salmon pinwheels are made by slicing a loaf of bread horizontally, flattening the slices with a rolling pin, and spreading them with smoked salmon mousse. Roll up each slice along its length, wrap tightly in plastic wrap, and chill for ten minutes (or until serving time) before slicing vertically into round pinwheels. To make the walnut and Brie sandwiches, be sure the Brie is ripe and softened at room temperature before spreading. With the scones, I love to serve clotted cream, an English specialty also sold as Devonshire cream. If clotted cream is not available, substitute crème fraîche or whipped heavy cream.

It is difficult to imagine a more elegant and memorable way to receive guests after a wedding.

Finger Sandwiches Served in a Bread Boule:
Smoked Salmon Mousse Pinwheels
Classic Cucumber
Egg Salad
Walnut and Brie
Deviled Ham with Tomato

Fresh Baked Scones
Strawberry and Apricot Jam
Clotted Cream
Madeleines

Wedding Cake with Fresh Berries and Crème Anglaise

Dry sherry
Ginger beer
Sparkling water
Earl Grey tea

A COCKTAIL RECEPTION

A cocktail party is a chic way to entertain friends after a small wedding. It also works well as a reception after a civil ceremony. This format allows you to entertain in a smaller space.

Invite friends for six P.M. and have waiters pass two kinds of retro cocktails to make things simple, like champagne cocktails and Manhattans, martinis, or Cosmopolitans. Have wine, soft drinks, sparkling water, and champagne available as well.

Fill the room with lush arrangements of flowers and hire a jazz combo—a pianist, saxophonist, stand-up bass player, and percussionist—to give an upbeat energy to the evening; or play your favorite jazz CDs. Create several different food stations so that guests can help themselves. Each station should be self-contained and feature a complete dish with forks, knives, napkins, and small plates, and the appropriate beverage.

Offer a side of presliced smoked salmon or gravlax with thin slices of party rye bread and a bottle of frozen vodka or aquavit with shot glasses on one table. Another food vignette might be an assortment of grilled gourmet flavored sausages, served in a chafing dish with plenty of toothpicks and an assortment of mustards in small bowls for dipping. On another buffet, arrange a beautiful platter of imported cheeses and crusty breads, along with a decanter of Port. In a central location, set out a lavish display of green and white vegetables served with a syrupy balsamic vinaigrette. If you'd like, waiters can pass a hot appetizer, such as seasoned pork sausage rolled in flaky puff pastry, on silver trays. Display the wedding cake, serving pieces and plates, a bottle of demi-sec champagne, and champagne flutes on a separate table.

This cocktail party is easy to do in a home setting because most of the items can be purchased rather than prepared, and everything can be done in advance (reheat the sausage rolls at the last minute). Also, the format doesn't require much serving or cleaning help. Guests love it because they can enjoy a complete dish on each buffet. You and your groom will love it because you can spend the evening with your guests enjoying a great party.

Sausage Rolls in Puff Pastry with Worcestershire Sauce (tray-passed)

Smoked Salmon with Rye Bread Station

Assorted Gourmet Flavored Sausage Station
with Dijon and Hot English Mustard

Crudité Station of White and Green Vegetables
with Balsamic Vinaigrette

Imported Cheese Station

Chocolate Wedding Cake with White Chocolate Frosting
Garnished with Fresh Raspberries

Champagne cocktails
Frozen vodka
Cosmopolitans
California Chardonnay
Vintage Port
Sparkling water

For this cocktail party, food was served from several different stations, accompanied by the appropriate beverage. Left: Stone crab claws with Meursault, a fine white Burgundy. Above, top to bottom: Cheeses with vintage Port; gravlax and smoked salmon with frozen vodka and aquavit; champagne and frozen vodka at the caviar bar.

AN ELEGANT COCKTAIL PARTY IN A PENTHOUSE APARTMENT

A dressy cocktail party where nearly all the food is passed by waiters is a highly civilized way to entertain, and it works particularly well in a small space, such as a city apartment. This sort of party is a sophisticated approach for a couple who wants something out of the ordinary for their wedding reception.

The food should be pure luxe—caviar, foie gras, smoked salmon, shrimp—all the delicacies that people love. Create two buffet stations for guests to visit, one offering smoked salmon and gravlax, the other showcasing a mound of jumbo shrimp on cracked ice with a trio of piquant sauces. Lest the menu be thought too light, fill it out with mini crab cakes and a crisp-crusted pissaladière, a lusty Provençal pizza, cut into tiny squares.

Toward the end of the party, gather your guests in the largest room for the cutting of the cake and a champagne toast.

Caviar in Demitasse Spoons

Fresh Foie Gras on Toasted Brioche with Fresh Chervil

Smoked Salmon and
Gravlax Station

Jumbo Poached Shrimp at a Buffet Station
Served with a Trio of Sauces:
Classic Cocktail Sauce
Green Chili Oil
Tomato Mayonnaise

Mini Crab Cakes with Tartar Sauce

Pissaladière with Olives and
Caramelized Sweet Onions

Vanilla Wedding Cake with Hazelnut Cream Filling

Champagne
Sparkling water
Frozen vodka
Coffee

A BUFFET-STYLE RECEPTION DINNER

A carefully planned buffet is a great way to entertain large numbers of guests at a dinner. Too often, buffets are loaded with several meat, fish, and poultry dishes, which means guests end up with a hodgepodge on their plates rather than a menu of foods that complement each other. As I have noted previously, I prefer to have several buffet stations that are visited separately.

Here is a menu for a multicourse dinner that is served buffet-style. Waiters direct guests to the appropriate buffet station, depending on the course that is being served. The first course features delicious assorted smoked fish, such as salmon, halibut, and sturgeon, beautifully arranged on platters and garnished with lemon slices. A piquant watercress salad in a lemony vinaigrette is served with the smoked fish, offering complementary colors, tastes, and textures. The main course buffet showcases grilled rock Cornish game hens with a zesty mango and lime chutney and two side dishes. After guests have enjoyed the first two courses, there is a break for dancing while the buffets are being changed over, one to offer cake, the other to offer Cognac and coffee.

First Course Buffet
Assorted Smoked Fish
(Salmon, Sturgeon, Trout, and Halibut)
with Watercress Salad and Lemon Vinaigrette
Washington State Dry Riesling

Main Course Buffet
Grilled Marinated Cornish Game Hens
with Mango and Lime Chutney
Wild Rice with Raisins and Cashews
Fresh Sweet Corn
California Sauvignon Blanc

Dessert Buffet
Dense Chocolate Wedding Cake with Espresso Filling,
Fresh Gooseberries, and Whipped Cream

Coffee
Cognac

A RECEPTION DINNER IN THE GARDEN UNDER A CANOPY

For an early-fall wedding in an outdoor setting on a ranch, farm, or vineyard serve a menu of hearty fare that reflects the season. During the cocktail hour, waiters can pass appetizers of barbecued prawns on lemongrass skewers, and grilled venison and shiitake mushrooms on rosemary skewers. When guests move in to dinner they are served a delicious trio of vegetable raviolis napped with three colorful sauces. Guests' appetites are whetted for the buffet by the sight and aroma of butterflied leg of lamb grilled on large barbecues and sliced to order. A casserole of delicious flageolets, which are a bit like lima beans, and a medley of bright green asparagus spears and tiny haricots verts, rounds out the main course. A salad of peppery arugula, fresh basil, and orange slices provides a refreshing contrast. For dessert, a vanilla wedding cake with a chocolate Grand Marnier filling will tempt your guests, especially when accompanied by a few slices of pink grapefruit that have been marinated in Grand Marnier, and a small scoop of rich chocolate mousse.

Appetizers
Barbecued Prawns, Scallops, and Shrimp
on Lemon-grass Skewers
Grilled Venison and Shiitake Mushrooms
on Rosemary Skewers

California Chardonnay
Sparkling water

First Course
Trio of Vegetable Raviolis
(Potato, Pumpkin, and Fresh Corn)
with a Trio of Red, Yellow, and Orange Bell Pepper Sauces
California Pinot Blanc

Main Course
Barbecued Butterflied Leg of Spring Lamb, Sliced to Order
Flageolet Beans
Medley of Asparagus and Haricots Verts
Baby Carrots with Cippoline Onions
Salad of Arugula and Fresh Basil with Orange Segments
in a Lime Vinaigrette
Crusty Breads with Fragrant Olive Oil and Olive Tapenade
California Pinot Noir

Dessert
Vanilla Wedding Cake
with Chocolate and Grand Marnier Filling
Garnished with Pink Grapefruit Segments
Marinated in Grand Marnier
Sparkling Vouvray

Coffee

RECEPTION DINNER—A FORMAL AFFAIR

Here is a menu for an elegant sit-down dinner that offers guests a choice of main course. The dinner begins with an impressive three-dimensional puff pastry box filled with asparagus tips, tomato, and prawns, a dish that is as visually interesting as it is delicious. For the second course, a light salad of baby lettuces is served with waiters circulating to each table to top the salads with spoonfuls of warm goat cheese soufflé. A choice of roasted whitefish or duck is offered for the main course. A warm apple tart with caramel sauce and a tiny crème brûlée makes a fitting dessert. The pièce de résistance is the cutting of the wedding cake. Guests may partake in a little slice or take home a piece, as they wish.

Appetizers
Artichoke Canapés
Warm Lobster Tartlets

Champagne
Sparkling water

First Course
Puff Pastry Box Filled with
Concassé of Asparagus Tips and Tomato
Served with Two Grilled Prawns
and a Saffron Beurre Blanc

Meursault

Second Course
Salad of Mâche, Baby Frisée, and Butter Lettuces
with Crispy Leeks,
Chardonnay Vinaigrette, and
Warm Goat Cheese Soufflé

Main Course
Roast Breast of Duck with a Grape and Port Wine Sauce
Potatoes Dauphinoise, Asparagus, and Green Beans
or Roasted Whitefish with a Scallion and Ginger Sauce
Medley of Rice, Carrot Flan

Latricières-Chambertin
or
Bâtard Montrachet

Dessert
Apple Tart with Homemade Vanilla Ice Cream,
Served with Caramel Sauce and Mini Crème Brûlée

Barsac

Vanilla Wedding Cake Served with Apricot Coulis,
Fresh Berries, and Mint
Chocolate Truffles and Almond Tuiles

Demi-sec champagne
Coffee

RECEPTION DINNER—A BUFFET SUPPER

If you are looking for an informal, fun way to entertain guests after a ceremony that is held later in the evening, like eight or nine P.M., here is an exotic party menu that is casual yet features delicious, sophisticated food.

Start with appetizers, like Baba Ghanoush, a Middle Eastern chopped eggplant dip, which are passed on trays during the cocktail hour. Follow with a buffet supper that showcases an impressive whole oven-roasted sirloin of beef with a shiitake mushroom Bordelaise sauce and intriguing side dishes with plenty of flavor. The salad of delicate baby frisée and Boston lettuce is enriched with toasted walnuts, blue cheese, and thinly sliced ripe pears. The finale of the evening's menu is a delicious lemon poppy seed wedding cake. Who could resist?

Appetizers
Baby Potatoes with Baba Ghanoush
Peking Duck Pancakes with Plum Sauce
Swordfish Kabobs with a Soy Marinade
Parmesan Toasts with Prosciutto
Mini Crab Cakes with Tartar Sauce
Italian Pinot Grigio
Dolcetto d'Alba

Supper Buffet
Whole Oven-Roasted Sirloin of Beef
with Shiitake Mushroom Bordelaise Sauce
Medley of Fava Beans, Pearl Onions, Haricots Verts, and Petits Pois
Garlic Mashed Potatoes
Barbaresco

Salad of Baby Frisée (Curly Endive) and Boston Lettuce
with Toasted Walnuts, Blue Cheese, and Pears

Dessert
Lemon Poppy Seed Cake with Bittersweet Chocolate Ganache Filling
and White Chocolate Frosting
Served on Vanilla Crème Anglaise
with Fresh Berries and Mint
Biscotti

Sparkling water
Moscato d'Asti
Demitasse coffee

A SMALL DINNER IN A RESTAURANT'S PRIVATE ROOM

For a small wedding and a celebration with close friends, what could be more pleasant than a dinner reception either in your home or in a restaurant's private room? It is the most intimate type of reception that you can have. And it's easy. Simply rent or borrow a couple of elegant linen tablecloths. Create a pair of beautiful floral centerpieces that don't obstruct guests' views, and fill the tables with votive candles. The mood of the evening is set with vintage recordings of jazz artists from the thirties and forties.

Pull out all the stops and serve champagne from start to finish. Begin the dinner with tray-passed hors d'oeuvres of smoked salmon and flutes of a bone-dry brut. Serve a richly flavored but light lobster consommé as the first course, accompanied by a vintage bubbly. Roasted veal loin with a rosemary jus, and accompanied by a flavorful rosé champagne, is an outstanding main course. The meal is capped with a warm tart filled with fresh figs and served with crème fraîche. Then, move guests to a den or lounge for the cutting of the cake and demi-sec (slightly sweet) champagne. The toasting begins. What could be more festive?

Hors d'Oeuvres
Sliced Smoked Salmon on Crispy Potato Rounds

First Course
Lobster Consommé with Julienned Lobster Claw
and Shaved Black Truffles
Vintage champagne

Main Course
Roasted Veal Loin with Rosemary Jus
Timbale of Wild Mushrooms and Basmati Rice
Zucchini and Carrot Ribbons
Rosé champagne

Dessert
Warm Fig Tart with Crème Fraîche
Angel Food Wedding Cake
with Rum Butter Cream

Sparkling water
Brut champagne non-vintage
Demi-sec champagne

WEDDING CAKES

T he three most important questions asked about a wedding are, one: What did the bride wear?

Two: What did they serve?

Three: What was the cake like?

The wedding cake is the crowning glory, the signature of your wedding. I always design the cake last, after all the other elements of the wedding have been planned. Be sure to book the baker early and specify the number of people the cake is to serve, but leave the design of the cake open until you have refined and completed all the other design elements of the wedding.

Wedding cakes are usually incredibly elaborate. Many have four or more layers, often separated by pillars and festooned with filigree and spun sugar. Ornamentation includes fresh flowers or sugar-paste blossoms, marzipan fruits, candied violets, piped swirls of frosting, ribbon, and lacework. Sometimes, the wedding cake doesn't look like a cake at all, but instead might resemble a stack of sumptuously wrapped presents, an abundant basket of flowers, or a miniature Victorian gazebo.

The cake is very much like the bridal gown: it can easily look overproduced. Cakes decorated with multiple elements, such as tiers, columns, lacework, flowers, ribbons, and beading, can look fussy. Using just one or two types of ornamentation makes for an elegantly designed wedding cake.

When deciding on your cake, consider all the elements of your wedding. What time of day is the meal being served? What will the weather be like? An outdoor reception on a warm, humid August evening is not the occasion for a fragile many-tiered confection of butter cream and spun sugar.

How large is the room where the cake will be displayed, and how high is the ceiling? The scale of the cake in the room is extremely important. A large room with high ceilings requires a cake with height and scale. One option for additional height is to add a dummy layer that is frosted and matches the thick, stacked layers of the rest of the cake. Or, place the cake on a raised platform for added height.

How formal is your wedding? What is the menu for the meal? A multicourse gourmet dinner calls for a refined cake, perhaps one filled with a lemon mousse or liqueur-flavored butter cream.

Your cake continues the visual theme of your wedding in its reflection of colors, motifs, and style. If the style of your wedding is baroque with extensive use of gold-colored fabrics and props and elaborate flower arrangements, the design of your cake should reflect that level of elaboration. A sleek, contemporary wedding style calls for a cake with clean, pristine lines.

The location of your reception can provide a visual theme. If you are being married at a winery, surrounded by vineyards, your baker might drape the cake with marzipan grapes, sugared grapes, or even with real miniature champagne grapes and trails of variegated ivy.

Your florist can decorate your wedding cake with fresh blossoms and greenery. Cakes adorned with the same fresh flowers that the bride carried in her bouquet are particularly beautiful. (Check with your

A summer garden cake, decorated by Sylvia Weinstock with a profusion of pastillage flowers, including Leonidas and Sahara roses and lily of the valley. The latticework, created with brown piped butter cream, matched the baskets of flowers that were used as centerpieces on the dining tables.

Left: Wendy Kromer frosted this three-tiered cake with crimped white fondant. Violets, sweet peas, Johnny-jump-ups, roses, lilacs, and baby's breath, made of pastillage and royal icing, decorated each tier. *Top left:* Another Wendy Kromer cake covered in Wedgwood blue fondant with fondant bows and swags and a bouquet of pastillage wildflowers on top. *Top center:* A traditional three-tiered cake, decorated with a white butter cream icing by Hansen's Cakes. *Top right:* Polly Schoonmaker's cutting-edge, whimsical wedding cake decorated with tinted fondant. *Middle left:* Another Polly Schoonmaker cake with hand-painted grapes, peaches, berries, and greens on white butter cream. *Middle center:* Laura Moniz created an Indian-style layered cake iced in purple and pink butter cream, decorated with gilded swags and gold dragées. *Middle right:* A five-tiered cake, with white chocolate draping by Linda Goldsheft. *Bottom left:* Jane Lockhart of Sweet Lady Jane made this simple four-tiered cake decorated with pastillage calla lilies. *Bottom center:* A dramatic cake strewn with brilliantly colored pastillage flowers, draped in pastillage gold tassels, and decorated with piped butter cream by Sylvia Weinstock. *Bottom right:* Linda Goldsheft created this imposingly tall cake with fabric-like draping of white chocolate on the corners.

florist to be sure the flowers have not been sprayed with pesticides or fumigants, and always remove the flowers before serving the cake.) A colorful floral motif may be hand-painted onto the frosting of a cake, and a talented artist may even be able to replicate a floral fabric pattern. A skilled pastry artist can also duplicate the look of actual three-dimensional flowers in pastillage (sugar paste), although this is considerably more expensive than using fresh flowers.

Wedding cakes can be utterly sleek and modern, if that's your style. For a contemporary wedding that had an all-white color scheme, we took a minimalist approach to the flowers and used only snow white calla lilies and clouds of gypsophila. We then created a very simple four-layer cake enrobed in creamy rolled fondant, with the top layer on short columns. The cake had absolutely no ornamentation save for translucent wide white silk ribbon wrapped around each layer and a cluster of pastillage calla lilies among the columns. It was displayed on the cake table surrounded by gypsophila.

As you work with your baker to develop the design for your cake, review sketches and diagrams that show the cake's finished dimensions. After you have approved the design, the contract with your baker should include a diagram with dimensions, to make sure the finished cake will be the size you expect.

Wedding cakes should be fresh and moist. Famed New York cake artist Sylvia Weinstock advises that cakes should be baked no earlier than twenty-four hours before they are to be served. She also suggests tasting samples at the bakery, and asking specifically, "Am I going to have a cake that tastes like this?"

Bakers now make wedding cakes in a variety of colors and flavors, and layer them with delicious fillings, too. In fact, chocolate, formerly used only in the groom's cake (traditionally a smaller cake that was displayed with the main wedding cake), is now one of the most frequently requested flavors for wedding cakes. Although it used to be quite popular, the groom's cake is seldom seen at today's weddings. The legend is that a single woman who takes home a slice of the groom's cake and puts it under her pillow will dream of the man she will marry.

There are many ways to frost wedding cakes. If you want a completely smooth surface, the baker might use either white chocolate, which drapes beautifully, or rolled fondant, which gives the smooth look of alabaster. Detailed decoration is often done with royal icing, a type of frosting that hardens upon exposure to air and looks like fine porcelain. The moistest frosting is butter cream, which must be refrigerated until the cake is ready to be displayed.

The frosting you choose affects the type of cake you can serve. Neither fondant nor royal icing can be refrigerated, which limits the kind of ingredients that can be used to fill the cake. White chocolate may be refrigerated, and butter cream must be refrigerated. Use perishable custard, whipped cream, and mousse fillings only with cakes that will be refrigerated.

DRESSING THE CAKE TABLE

The table that displays the cake should be decorated beautifully. Use the same linens (or complementary ones) as on your dining tables, perhaps layering the cloths and pinning up sections with fresh flower corsages, or adding swags of tulle or lace. The table can also be strewn with rose petals or sprays of flowers. Arrangements of sugared fruits, such as champagne grapes, miniature pears, or cherries, give a beautiful look as well. On a large table, set a bottle of champagne in a gleaming silver ice bucket and add a grouping of champagne flutes. An heirloom cake knife tied with a satin bow is an elegant touch.

A sturdy wheeled table is useful because it can be easily moved to the dance floor for the cake cutting. Like any focal point in the room, the cake table should be well illuminated.

TAKING THE CAKE HOME

It is considered good luck for guests at the wedding to take home a small slice of cake. Your caterer can arrange for slices to be packaged in cellophane and tied with ribbon for your guests.

It is also traditional for the bride and groom to save a slice, or perhaps the top tier of the cake, freeze it, and share it on their first anniversary. Make sure that arrangements have been made in advance if you choose to save the top tier. It would be disappointing to find that the top tier has been thrown away when you were expecting to take it home.

CAKE LOGISTICS

Moving a wedding cake is a job for professionals only. The cake baker should also be the cake deliverer. Preferably, the baker should deliver the cake to the exact spot where it will be displayed. Brief your baker fully; he or she needs to know about any stairs that must be negotiated and how close to the site the delivery vehicle can park. If inexperienced people try to move a wedding cake, disaster may ensue!

Top left: This lavishly ornamented, five-tiered cake, with each layer on risers, was created by Donald Wressell. It was decorated with crystallized sugared grapes, fresh roses, and gold ribbons made from spun sugar. Top right: White chocolate draping covered this four-foot-high, six-tiered cake by Linda Goldsheft. Bottom left: A five-tiered cake from Polly Schoonmaker was covered with fondant decorated in a parquet pattern reminiscent of Italian Renaissance interiors, beaded with gold dragées, and strewn with fresh flowers. Bottom right: Laura Moniz created this six-tiered cake, which was frosted in butter cream with piping that matched the tablecloths.

Linda Goldsheft, a talented baker who owns The Cake Studio in Orange County, California, advises brides to insist that their cake be made of top-quality ingredients, such as real butter and cream. Some bakers cut corners and use vegetable shortening in wedding cakes.

Choose an experienced professional to bake your wedding cake. Cake disasters almost invariably occur because the cake was prepared by an inexperienced baker. With their multilayered structure, weight, and ornamentation, wedding cakes must be carefully constructed and internally reinforced. This allows the cake to withstand the stress of being moved and to hold up for several hours without refrigeration.

Sometimes the baker may supplement the display cake with the same flavor of frosted sheet cake that is kept in the kitchen and pre-plated. This allows you to serve a large number of people in a short period of time. If you desire a large, impressive cake, the baker may be able to create a dummy layer on the bottom that is frosted to resemble a real layer but just provides support and height. Each of these options will help lower the cost of the display cake.

For all but the most formal affairs, it's perfectly appropriate to serve the wedding cake as dessert. Make it look like a fabulous treat by decorating the plate. Drizzle the plate with peach, strawberry, passion fruit, or raspberry coulis, or crème anglaise. Serve the cake with fresh strawberries, raspberries, or any favorite fruit. Lightly dust cocoa powder, edible gold dust, powdered sugar, or powdered espresso coffee over the plate, or garnish the plate with a few candied violets.

Wedding cake is rarely the only dessert at a formal dinner. If a separate dessert is planned, it would be served before the cutting of the cake. Another option is to include the cake as part of a dessert assortment. Take an oversized plate and serve a small slice of wedding cake and sauce, an almond tuile with homemade ice cream or sorbet, a mini crème brûlée or mini flourless chocolate cake, a few berries, and one or two cookies. Each guest receives an individual dessert medley.

After the dessert and cake, a little treat, such as a small dish of fine chocolates or an assortment of tiny, elegant cookies, is a great way to finish off a meal.

Left: A Linda Goldsheft creation draped in quilted fondant dusted with pearlescence. Tiny pastillage violets dotted the quilting. Below: Simple in an ornate setting, this five-tiered cake, made by Linda Goldsheft, was covered with celadon fondant. Ivory swirled detailing was done in butter cream, with clusters of fresh roses in autumnal colors.

WEDDING CAKE FLAVORS

Most professional bakers offer wedding cakes in a variety of flavors with delicious fillings. Wedding cakes can have layers in different flavors. Here are some of my favorite flavors for cakes, frostings, and fillings:

Lemon cake with lemon mousse filling

Lemon pound cake with walnut cream filling

Chocolate cake with hazelnut cream filling

Fruitcake with a brandy-laced filling

Chocolate cake with white chocolate filling

White chocolate cake with a filling of fresh strawberries and whipped cream

Poppyseed cake filled with passion fruit mousse

THE ENGLISH TRADITION

British wedding cakes traditionally are rich, heavy fruitcakes that are baked months in advance of the wedding, soaked liberally with brandy, frosted with marzipan, and elaborately decorated with royal icing. The cake then ripens over a period of weeks. The brandy keeps the fruitcake moist and flavorful.

THE FRENCH TRADITION

A traditional French pastry for weddings is the *croquembouche*, an impressive pyramid of profiteroles, or cream puffs, filled with pastry cream.

PASTRY TERMS

Butter cream: a rich combination of butter and sugar, butter cream may be used as frosting and filling for cakes

Candied violets: actual violet blooms that are sugar-frosted and used as edible decorations

Dragées: the French term for small gold and silver shot that are used to decorate cakes and cookies (be sure these are the edible kind)

Fondant, or rolled fondant: a confectionary icing that is rolled like pastry dough and produces a very smooth finish on the cake

Ganache: a combination of chocolate, butter, and cream, which can be made in a range of thicknesses

Génoise: the French term for a classic, firm white cake made with butter, eggs, sugar, and flour

Marzipan: a confection of almond paste that is often colored and shaped to resemble miniature fruits, or used as a thin layer between cake and royal icing

Pastillage: a paste of sugar, cornstarch, and gelatin that can be used to sculpt realistic-looking flowers and other decorations

Royal icing: a cooked icing that air-dries to a hard, porcelain-like finish

Spun sugar: gossamer-like strands of golden caramel that are made by dipping a fork or multipronged tool into melted sugar and whipping it rapidly in the air to form filaments

THE CAKE CUTTING

Most brides and grooms wait too long to cut the cake. Don't wait until the very end of your reception to cut the cake, or half your guests may have left. If wedding cake is the dessert, the cake cutting should occur when dessert would reasonably be served (after the main course and a short dance set). The cake cutting is a signal that the fun has just begun.

Traditionally, the bride and groom feed each other the first bites of the cake. In some circles, this has evolved into a circus-like ritual where the bride and groom mash handfuls of cake into each other's faces. I find that custom distasteful. You spent hours getting ready for the most special day of your life—you don't want to end up with cake all over your face. These first bites of cake should be traded tenderly, as a gesture of how the bride and groom will treat each other in their new life together.

I'm going to let you in on a little secret. The key factor that really makes or breaks a party is almost always ignored by people putting on a wedding. It's something that everyone has access to and it doesn't cost a dime. It's *timing*.

How often have you attended a wedding that started at six in the evening; the bride came down the aisle after seven; the cocktail reception ran from eight until nine-thirty; and dinner was finally put in front of you at ten-thirty at night? By midnight, you've been there for six hours, and they haven't even cut the cake. Your energy level has dropped and maybe you've had too much to drink. This is the profile of many weddings where issues like timing and the elements that go into creating a good party have been ignored.

The quality of time people spend at a wedding is far more important than the quantity of time. As the bride and groom, the host and hostess of this party, it is up to you to ensure that your guests will enjoy themselves. Think of it as taking your guests on a journey for the day. You want the journey to be interesting and full of lots of fun and laughter. In order to do that, you need to get a pace and a rhythm going, and control it with the use of food, drink, music, and a strong sense of timing.

Parties need to be kept in motion. With a wedding reception, which may involve a succession of events such as a photo session for the bridal party, a cocktail hour, dinner, dancing, speeches, and the cake cutting, it's absolutely critical that you plan the timing and stay to a schedule.

If guests are invited for a seven P.M. ceremony, start the ceremony by seven-fifteen or seven-twenty at the very latest. Once the ceremony is over, if there is a cocktail reception it should last no longer than forty-five minutes to an hour. Keep the rest of the evening moving on a schedule, so that there aren't periods of downtime when guests are waiting for the next event to happen. *Guests don't notice when timing is working well; they only notice when it's not.*

THE SCHEDULE OF EVENTS

How do you keep a party moving so everything unfolds before guests have a chance to think about what comes next? Create a written schedule of events that allows you to control the pace of the party.

The schedule of events is the most important and least expensive tool that I use to create incredible parties. I've employed it for every party and wedding I've ever done. Some schedules for simple weddings, such as a civil ceremony followed by a cocktail party, are a page long; others, for elaborate, large celebrations, run four to five pages.

Begin framing the schedule as soon as you know the basics: the time of the ceremony and the time of the reception. Then, flesh out the schedule as you meet with the officiant at your ceremony and each of your vendors. With the officiant, you'll determine the timing of the ceremony from start to finish. With the florist, you'll agree on the delivery times for the flowers and the hour by which all flowers are to be installed and broken down at the end of the evening. With the caterer, you'll set times for the cocktail party, meal service, and cake cutting, including setup and breakdown. With the band, you'll determine when they are to begin playing, when the breaks occur, when the energy is to be highest on the dance floor, and the latest time to which they'll play without incurring overtime charges. All this information goes on the written

SAMPLE SCHEDULE OF EVENTS

This schedule was developed for a large church wedding with a reception at a club. Note that because the reception site would not permit access to the ballroom until the day of the reception, the installation of the elaborate decor began at one minute past midnight the morning of the wedding day.

Friday   Gift baskets delivered to guest hotel rooms. Baskets to contain welcome note, weekend itinerary, map to rehearsal dinner, fresh fruit, and bottled water.

Saturday

5:00 P.M.	Water and glasses ready for wedding rehearsal
5:30 P.M.	Rehearsal at church
7:00 P.M.	Rehearsal over—guests proceed to restaurant for dinner

Sunday

12:01 A.M.	Installation of decor begins at reception site: carpeting, drapery, wall panels
10:00 A.M.	Food and beverages ready for bride and bridesmaids (mineral water and fresh fruit)
	Florist delivers to reception site and begins installation
10:45 A.M.	Florist delivers to setup room at church and begins floral arch
11:00 A.M.	Bridesmaids arrive at bride's home
	Assistant arrives with dresses
	Makeup artist and hairstylist arrive for bride, bridesmaids
12:00 Noon	Lunch is served to bride, mother, and bridesmaids
12:30 P.M.	Photographer arrives at bride's home for shots of everyone getting ready
1:00 P.M.	Photos of bride, mother and father, and bridesmaids—shot list provided by bride
	Personal flowers delivered to home
	Lunch is served to groom and groomsmen at hotel
	Church available after morning services
1:30 P.M.	Chorus arrives for rehearsal
2:00 P.M.	Photographer to finish bridesmaid shots and proceed to church for groom and groomsmen
	Limo #1: arrives for bride and her father
	Limo #2: arrives for bridesmaids
	Videographer arrives
2:15 P.M.	Limo #1: departs for church with bride and her father
	Limo #2: departs for church with bridesmaids
	Bridal dressing room at church set with water and fresh fruit
2:30 P.M.	Limo #1: arrives at church with bride and her father, then returns to bride's home for another pickup
	Limo #2: arrives at church with bridesmaids, then to hotel for another pickup
2:40 P.M.	Groom and groomsmen arrive at church
	Groomsmen photo session
	Sign-in table with guest book ready in entryway of church
2:45 P.M.	Limo #1: arrives at bride's home to pick up other members of wedding party
	Sommeliers arrive club
2:50 P.M.	Limo #2: arrives at hotel for others in wedding party
2:55 P.M.	Limo #1: leaves for church with others in wedding party
3:00 P.M.	Limo #2: departs hotel for church
	Chorus in place
	Quartet in place
3:00 P.M.	Candles ready, bow set across aisle, reserved seating cards on chairs

schedule, which is then distributed to each vendor. The schedule should be given to your vendors well in advance of your wedding, so that they can get back to you with any problems they foresee or changes that need to be made. The schedule gives you the confidence that everyone is "working off the same page."

As you put the schedule together, you may begin to notice problem areas: things that appear to be taking too much time, or gaps that need to be filled. In that case, you can make adjustments and continue to refine them. Better to think through and plan the timing of the party in advance than face an unexpected delay or lull with a hundred guests in the room!

Keep in mind one fact about large events. The more guests you have, the more time it will take to move them from one place to another. That is why the cocktail "hour" should actually run only forty-five minutes, because it takes fifteen minutes to move guests in to dinner.

Unless your wedding is a very small one, a production meeting should be held two to three days before the wedding on-site with all your vendors: wedding planner, caterer, photographer, florist, valet parker, lighting company, rental company, bandleader, and any other individuals who need to be familiar with the site and the schedule. The on-site production meeting allows everyone to walk through the plans for the wedding, and is an opportunity to address any problems or concerns before the big day and adjust the schedule of events accordingly.

Managing the schedule of events is a role for the wedding consultant, caterer, or a friend or relative who has good organizational skills and who is willing to help you on your wedding day. As long as the schedule is well understood by all participants, enforcing it is a matter of keeping one eye on the schedule and the other on the clock. As each event occurs, the coordinator can have a quick word with the person responsible for the next activity on the schedule.

The result of following a schedule is the party moves like clockwork. Guests are swept along by the rhythm. Every moment of their time at your wedding is planned in advance and filled with excitement and energy. That makes for a great party.

Of course, while timing is crucial to a successful wedding, there are other elements that need to be addressed. The tools that lay the foundation for a fabulous party include room layout, seating, lighting, designing the flow of the party, and music. Taken separately, these may seem like unimportant details, but I assure you, when they come together and work in harmony, they'll infuse your party with energy. In the pages that follow, you'll learn how to orchestrate these elements into a wonderful celebration of your wedding.

CONSIDER YOUR GUESTS

Before discussing the elements of a great party, it is important to emphasize that no consideration should come ahead of guest comfort. Aesthetics should never prevail over function. You may have the most beautiful floral centerpieces, but if you have neglected to provide adequate heating in your outdoor tent, your guests will never even notice the flowers.

No compromises should ever be made in guest comfort. This means that basic elements such as heating, air conditioning, lighting, nearby parking, adequate restrooms, and plenty of good food and beverages must be provided. You might think it unnecessary to make such an obvious statement, but then you might be surprised to see how uncomfortable and unhappy guests can be at a midsummer wedding outdoors

	Wedding cake delivered to reception site
	Videographer ready
3:10 P.M.	Limo #1: arrives at church
3:15 P.M.	Limo #2: arrives at church
	Chorus begins
	Groomsmen to waiting area
3:30 P.M.	Invitation time—guests are seated from the sides
3:35 P.M.	Groomsmen to leave waiting area and move to front of church for entrance
3:45 P.M.	Ceremony commences
	Procession music: Pachelbel Canon in D Minor—played by string quartet
	Grandmothers escorted down aisle and seated in first row
	Parents of groom down aisle
	Bride's mother down aisle
	Minister, groom, and best man proceed from choir door
	Groomsmen
	Bridesmaids
	Matron of honor
	Two ring bearers down aisle
	Two flower girls down aisle
	Church bells
	Music: "Wedding March"
	Bride and father down aisle
	Ritual commences:
	Lord's Prayer
	Readings
	Chorus to sing after reading
	Bride's mother and groom's mother to light candles
	Recessional: change to upbeat music
	Area set for chorus with fruit juice, water, and fruit
4:15 P.M.	Bridal party proceeds to waiting area
	Guests depart church
4:25 P.M.	Bridal party to altar for formal photo session
	Videographers ready at ceremony area for a few minutes
	Piano, bass, and sax in place at reception site
4:30 P.M.	Limos arrive at church to transport wedding party
	Staff at sign-in table set with seating cards
	Guests begin to arrive at reception site
	Waiters ready with silver trays of pre-poured champagne, white wine, red wine, and mineral water
	Videographer at reception site
4:45 P.M.	Limos depart church for reception site—don't forget bridal clothing and handbags
4:50 P.M.	Limos arrive at reception site
4:55 P.M.	Parents join cocktail reception
5:10 P.M.	Bride and groom photo session on grounds of reception site
5:20 P.M.	Full band in place and playing in ballroom
5:30 P.M.	Guests are escorted to ballroom
5:45 P.M.	Band announces bride and groom
	First dance: "Kiss from a Rose"
	Parents of bride and groom invited to join
	Bridal party invited to join
	Family and friends invited to join
	Guests invited to join—music to be upbeat
6:15 P.M.	Wine and water served
	Guests are invited to be seated
6:30 P.M.	First course is served

	Music—background only, five minutes
6:35 P.M.	Music breaks
	Father of bride makes welcome speech
6:37 P.M.	Music—background only
6:50 P.M.	Second course is served
7:05 P.M.	Music to pick up beat—build to first peak
7:35 P.M.	Main course is served
	Music—background, only
8:00 P.M.	Music: Father-daughter dance—"Sunrise Sunset"
	Music changes to upbeat with vocal and builds to second peak
8:50 P.M.	Cake cutting—bride and groom speak
9:00 P.M.	Dessert and cake are served
9:10 P.M.	Music picks up tempo for final peak
9:45 P.M.	Bouquet and garter toss
	Limo #1: arrives for bride and groom
	Limo #2: arrives for parents, grandparents
10:00 P.M.	Limo #1: bride and groom depart for hotel
	Limo #2: parents, grandparents depart
10:10 P.M.	Guests begin to depart
	Band finishes; quiet recorded background music commences

Monday

8:00 A.M.	Load out begins
	Liquor store collects leftover beverages
8:30 A.M.	Lighting company dismantles lighting
	Florist removes floral vessels and props
9:00 A.M.	Rental company removes rentals

where no canopies, umbrellas, or shady trees are available, or at a club where there are insufficient restroom facilities for female guests. In making decisions about the flow and timing of your party, how your space is laid out, when your meal will be served, and the services and amenities available at your space, keep these key issues uppermost in your mind.

If your wedding will take place outdoors, or in any indoor space that does not frequently house large events, be sure that your electrical supply is adequate. Find out how much electricity your caterer, band, lighting company, and any other power users will require, then check to see if the power supply will handle the load. At many outdoor weddings, a generator is needed, either to augment the power supply or to serve as an emergency backup. It may seem expensive to have a generator on hand, but it could save the day.

Always have a contingency plan if weather may be a factor in your guests' comfort. If you are planning an outdoor wedding under a tent during a season when the weather might turn suddenly cold or rainy, be sure that the tent has sides and that heaters are available, or that you have an alternate heated location.

ROOM LAYOUT

The way you lay out the space in which you'll hold your reception has a powerful influence on how the party moves.

Think first about the entrance to the space and put yourself in the position of a guest entering the room. Remember that the central focal point of the room creates that all-important first impression. Your eyes should be immediately drawn to what you want the guests to see: the cake, the band playing, waiters holding trays of champagne, beautiful illuminated floral centerpieces. Lay out your room with this in mind.

The key elements in the room should be placed with a sense of symmetry. The dance floor is the focal point of the room, the energy hub of the party. The bridal party table or tables are best placed next to the dance floor in the center of the room, with all the other tables filling in around it. Sometimes, the bridal party is seated along one side of a long rectangular table that is often raised on a dais. I feel this looks as though they are seated in a shop window. I prefer to seat the bridal party at a large round or oval table, which is more conducive to conversation. Or, the wedding party can be seated at the same size table as guests, but set off in some way, such as with a larger centerpiece, a canopy, or chair-back garlands for the bride and groom.

If you have a very large bridal party, you needn't seat the entire party at one table. Sometimes it is fun to split the group among three tables, with the bride and groom either seated with their parents or grandparents, or with their attendants and groomsmen. Members of the bridal party and their spouses, partners, or dates should be seated at the same table.

At some weddings, you will see what is called the sweetheart table, a table for two for the bride and groom. I feel that the wedding reception is a time to celebrate with your nearest and dearest friends and family. There will be plenty of time for just the two of you on your honeymoon.

Make the wedding cake a focal point in the room. It's a fabulous creation—why not make sure guests can admire it throughout the evening! You can choose to place the cake right in the middle of the room, close to the entrance, or next to the dance floor—wherever you place it, light it so that guests' attention is drawn to it. A microphone should be made accessible to the table for the cake cutting and the bride and groom's thank-you speech to the guests.

Plan the location of the buffets and the bars so that they are evenly

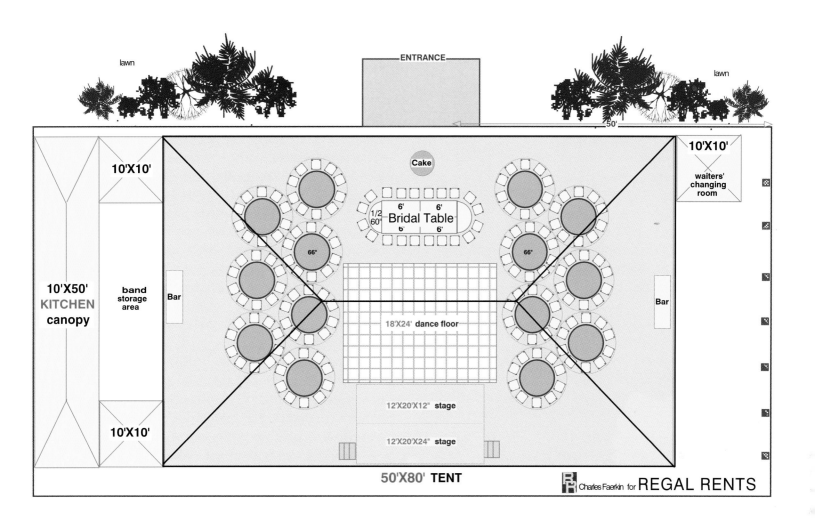

ENTRANCE

lawn

lawn

50'

10'X10'

10'X10'
waiters'
changing
room

Cake

10'X10'

10'X50'
KITCHEN
canopy

band
storage
area

Bar

66"

1/2
60'

6' | 6'
Bridal Table
6' | 6'

66"

Bar

18'X24' dance floor

12'X20'X12" **stage**

12'X20'X24" **stage**

50'X80' TENT

Charles Faerkin for REGAL RENTS

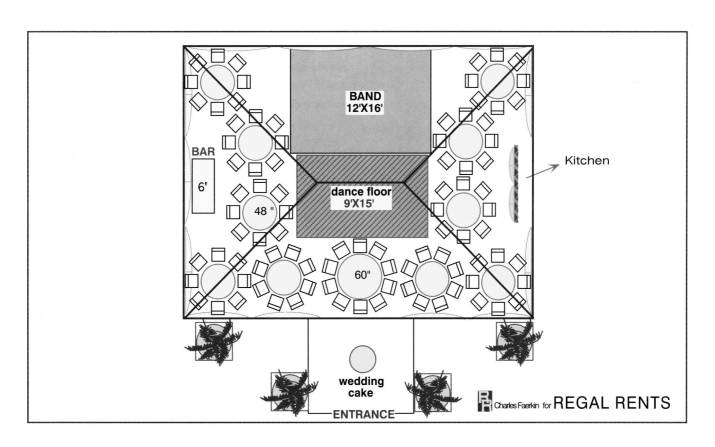

BAND
12'X16'

Kitchen

BAR

6'

48 "

dance floor
9'X15'

60"

wedding
cake

ENTRANCE

Charles Faerkin for REGAL RENTS

Top: Under a canopy on a tennis court, guests were seated ten to a sixty-six-inch round table, with tables spaced closely to encourage conversation and intimacy. Bottom: The wedding cake was placed in the center of the entrance to the tent to make it a focal point. Guests were seated at smaller forty-eight-inch round tables to ensure an intimate dinner.

spaced around the room. It is a good idea to have a pair of buffets and bars rather than one of each. It helps avoid lines and creates symmetry in the room.

Spacing between tables is important. When faced with a large ballroom that holds five hundred and a guest list that numbers three hundred, your instinct may be to spread tables around to fill the space. That just leaves a lot of desolate empty space between tables. I think guests should be kept close together. It allows guests' collective energy to pass from one table to another. No matter how large the space may be, I cluster tables close together, illuminate them, and leave any empty area around the perimeter in darkness. The empty area disappears, and you are left with a party setting that is full of life, noise, and energy. Don't worry about the waiters; leave one to two feet between the chair backs and they will be able to get through.

Seating guests close to one another at the table breaks the ice and makes for easier conversation. I like to seat ten people at a sixty-inch round and eight at a fifty-four-inch round. For a formal dinner with multiple glasses and lots of silverware, you could use a seventy-two-inch round for ten to twelve. When possible, I try to avoid seating twelve people at a table, because it is more difficult to create group energy while dining.

Nowhere is it written that you must use standard-size dinner tables. Playing with the table size changes the dynamics of the party. At one small reception for seventy guests, I could have fit everyone easily at sixty-inch rounds. I opted to seat guests close to each other at small fifty-four-inch rounds. The room felt a bit crowded, creating intimacy in the space and giving the party great energy.

For a cocktail reception or informal dinner, you might consider café-style seating with thirty-, thirty-six-, or forty-two-inch rounds and no place settings at the tables. Or, use taller stand-up bar tables, with or without bar stools. This approach is informal and fun, and it's easier for guests to mingle with one another.

At any cocktail reception, it is not necessary to provide seating for all the guests. My rule of thumb is to provide seating for all elderly or disabled guests, plus additional seating for 20 or 30 percent of the guests.

TENTS

Tent technology—if there is such a phrase—has taken off. Tents used to be simple affairs, with a central pole and framework over which canvas was draped. Today, tents can be as simple or elaborate as the client desires. A creative tent designer can construct not only a tented ballroom, but additional structures such as walkways, entrances, anterooms, and rotundas to house various aspects of your reception.

The options are virtually unlimited. You might create an anteroom to showcase your wedding cake at the entrance to your main tent. You could add a tented open-air cigar lounge, filled with sofas and chairs, to your reception. A smaller tent may also be used to house portable toilets to make them more attractive.

A tent, which has a framework with a center pole, is different from a canopy, which has side poles but no center pole. The advantage of working with a tent is that the ceiling is much higher.

A canopy or tent provides a completely neutral, blank space in which to create your environment. On a warm day or evening, you might prefer to leave your tent open, with no sides. Or, you could add tent sides, either clear or made of canvas. Depending on the effect you are seeking, you can make a tent look almost like a permanent structure by adding inset windows and interior wall panels covered with fabric. The high ceiling of a tent gives you the option of swagging it with fabric or hanging chandeliers. If you choose not to decorate the tent's interior, ask your rental company to wrap the metal tent poles in plastic or fabric, which enhances the look of the space inexpensively.

Proper flooring is important for the comfort and safety of your guests. If the ground beneath your tented area is uneven or wet, you may want to consider laying a subfloor that can then be covered with wall-to-wall carpeting, turf carpeting, sisal, or parquet. If wetness may be a problem but you do not wish to incur the expense of installing a subfloor, your rental company can cover the ground with heavy plastic and lay carpeting on top of that.

When using a tent, keep in mind the need to check on and comply with all local ordinances. Many municipalities require a permit to erect a reception tent.

WORKING WITH A PHOTOGRAPHER OR VIDEOGRAPHER

Wedding photos or videos are wonderful keepsakes. A good photographer or videographer captures the spontaneous moments that make a wedding unforgettable. To be sure you get everything you want, negotiate in advance with your photographer or videographer and be specific about your needs. Do you want color only, sepia and color, or black and white and color? What percentage of each? Does the photographer hand-tint? Does the price include an album? Wedding photographers often offer packages at varying price levels that include a range of prints; what is the cost of ordering prints beyond the number included in the package? Be sure you understand exactly what you are getting for your money.

You should also specify the style of photography you desire. Maybe you don't want dozens of posed portraits and would prefer to have your wedding documented in a photojournalistic style, with candids taken throughout the evening. It is important to select a photographer who specializes in that style and to communicate your preferences up front.

For formal photos, write up a list of the shots you need and give the list to the photographer. To save time, there may be several in the wedding party who can be photographed before the ceremony. The more shots you ask for, the longer the session will take and the more it will cost. An idea that saves time and money is to focus on getting *one* great shot of the entire wedding party. If you want candids of the cocktail party in addition to the formal shots of the wedding party, the photographer may need to bring an assistant to cover both if formals are going to take up all his or her time.

Be sure the arrival times are clearly understood. Find out whether the photographer or videographer is bringing any assistants. If you are having a formal wedding, it's wise to ask what the photographer and assistants will be wearing. They should be dressed appropriately for the level of formality of your party, and at a minimum should wear a dark suit or blazer and tie.

Ask who owns the proofs (the prints that the photographer provides, from which you select enlargements) and whether you can buy the negatives. Sometimes photographers retain the proofs and sell prints; others will sell negatives and you can have prints made inexpensively. Often you can arrange to purchase all the proofs, which make great gifts to send to the wedding party and your guests, if desired. For special gifts, these may be framed, or they can be placed in inexpensive cardboard folded frames that are available at many photo shops and mass merchants. The cardboard frames have the virtue of being easy to mail.

THE FLOW OF THE PARTY

You can enhance your celebration by knowing how to influence the natural flow of your party. Outdoor weddings can take advantage of the changing light as day turns into dusk and then into night. The pre-ceremony gathering takes place in the late afternoon; the ceremony at sunset; the cocktail hour at dusk; and the party at nighttime. Guests experience the magic as the outdoor light wanes and the candles and soft lighting begin to glow.

Moving guests from one area to another builds anticipation for what is to come and focuses the energy of the group. Before the ceremony, guests can gather outside the ceremony area and sip iced tea or sparkling water. Then, the ceremony can take place inside. After the ceremony, guests move to the cocktail area, then are ushered into the dinner. For a wedding at home, you might begin in the front garden, have the ceremony in front of the living room fireplace, hold the reception in the backyard, and cut the cake in the dining room.

Orchestrating the flow of a party is a bit like directing a film. You build to a climax or peak, then you're on to the next scene and building to another peak. Keep the momentum moving and your celebration will be a joyous one.

Receiving lines take a tremendous amount of time, particularly at a large wedding, and they tie up the key people, which dampens the energy of the party. I usually avoid them. It is much more natural for the bride, groom, and bridal party to circulate and greet guests during the cocktail hour and/or between courses at the dinner.

If you don't control it carefully, wedding photography can consume too much time. Plan ahead how many formal shots you want and keep in mind that it usually takes a minute and a half to two minutes per shot. Taking sixty shots will tie up the wedding party for at least an hour and a half. Better to concentrate on getting a good photo of the entire wedding party, send a copy to everyone in the shot, and let the wedding party have fun with the guests!

As you plan the flow, remember that you, the bride and groom, create energy. When it is time to move guests from the cocktail party into dinner, you and your groom should retire to a private area to spend an intimate moment or two together. Then, guests may be ushered into the party area, setting the stage to announce your entrance.

THE WALK-THROUGH

A day or two before the wedding, when all the preparations have been made and everything is ready for your big moment, take an hour and put yourself in the position of a guest at your wedding. Walk through everything that happens as that guest arrives. Think about every tiny detail. Where will the guest park? Is it easy to see where to proceed from the parking area? Is the pre-ceremony space easy to find? At the ceremony site, are there provisions for coats and wraps? Where are the restrooms?

Proceed in this manner through the ceremony and to the reception. Walk through every element of the guest's arrival at the reception. Consider whether the restrooms are easy to find, where guests will leave coats or purses, how they will find their tables, and where the phones are.

At every opportunity, ask yourself if there is anything that can be done

Top: On the honeymoon suite door, a note to the bride from the groom. Middle: The nuptial bed covered in rose petals; beside it, champagne chilling in an ice bucket and an array of sweet treats. Bottom: The honeymoon suite stocked with all the groom's favorite things.

REMEMBER THE NEIGHBORS

Part of being a good host is behaving thoughtfully to those who may be inconvenienced by your wedding. This is extremely important if your ceremony or reception is being held at a private home. Neighbors may be inconvenienced by delivery trucks, guest parking, or noise, particularly if the reception will run late into the evening. Think through whether your preparations will cause neighbors any inconvenience, and if so, how this can be avoided or minimized. If you wish, discuss the situation with the neighbors in advance. The day before the event, deliver a bottle of wine or some flowers with a short note expressing your good wishes and hopes that they are not unduly inconvenienced. Your thoughtful behavior will go a long way in smoothing over any problems.

SEATING

The best way to plan seating at your reception is the old-fashioned way: write every person's name on a three-by-five card and begin to group guests into tables of six, eight, or ten. This allows you to group names and move guests from one table to another easily. Once you have determined the seating, write it up on a master list on your personal computer.

Host cards tell guests their table assignment, while place cards go at each person's place setting. Once you have your master seating list, you can give it to a calligrapher or whoever is producing the host cards and/or place cards. At a small reception, waiters can pass the host cards on silver trays, or for larger parties, guests can pick up their host cards at the entrance of the reception area or during the cocktail reception. Be sure to have two extra host cards for each table so that when there are last-minute seating changes you will have an extra host card for guests who must be moved. If you are using a calligrapher, have him or her enclose a calligraphy pen and extra place cards and envelopes for last-minute changes.

WORKING WITH A HOTEL

When holding a function at a hotel, it is critical to find out the rules on setting up events, deliveries, parking, labor union rules, and outside services. Many hotels have restrictions on when events can be set up and deliveries made, and even which baker can be used. Some hotels are unionized and will not permit outside contractors to perform certain functions. Some hotels will permit outside contractors as long as they also work with the unionized hotel staff.

In dealing with hotels it is important to ask a lot of questions, because frequently there are surprises when the bill is presented. Hotels often charge for items or services that the client may not anticipate. Ask about charges for coat check, valet parking, room rental, audiovisual equipment, setup for the ceremony, a cake fee for an outside bakery, administration charges, and gratuities. It may or may not be possible to negotiate on some of these charges, but it's better to do it in advance than to be surprised when the bill is presented.

to make the guest more comfortable. Last, but not least, you might want to make sure that the honeymoon suite is confirmed and that the hotel is expecting you.

If you are a supremely talented planner, you may find there is nothing further to be done! Often, though, the walk-through results in your being able to foresee a potential problem and handle it well before guests arrive.

MUSIC

Music has an incredible effect on any gathering of people. It gives you the ability to control the energy and set the mood.

Decide whether to use live or recorded music, or some combination of the two. Live music is advantageous because musicians can instantly respond and change the tempo of the music. Pre-recorded music requires advance planning.

There should be music whenever your wedding guests enter a space. Cocktail party music should be upbeat and can range from lively jazz and standards to rhythm and blues. Recorded music will fill in the gap as guests are gathering for cocktails and the band is setting up in the dining room.

Consider using a music service or agent to book the band for your reception. If a problem arises with the band you have booked, the agent will be able to find a replacement. If you book directly, you risk a last-minute cancellation if a key musician has an emergency. Always ask if the band that is being recommended plays together regularly. A self-contained band usually has all their songs planned out and will give you the most professional sound. A pickup band that doesn't regularly play together may be less polished.

Arrange to see the band live before you book them, if possible. The way to ensure your music preferences and expectations are communicated to the band is to speak directly with the bandleader. That way, you can create a rapport with the person in charge of the music at your party.

A good bandleader understands energy and timing and can respond to the mood on the dance floor and pick just the right music to keep the party on course. Negotiate with the bandleader when the band will arrive, what they will wear, how many breaks they will take, how long the breaks are, and when they will occur. If the band is supposed to begin playing at seven-thirty P.M., they shouldn't still be setting up at seven-twenty-nine. When your guests enter the dining area, the band should already be *playing*. Better to keep the guests out of the room a few minutes longer than to have them enter a room with no music. Try to avoid having the band go on break just as guests are finishing their food and thinking about dancing, or when the dance floor is full and the party is really moving.

It is usually possible to pay extra for "continuous music," which means playing all evening with no breaks. This gives you ultimate control over the music at your party. However, it's also fine to fill in the breaks with recorded music. You can put together a selection of your favorites on tape, which can be played during breaks, or ask the band to provide recorded music for the breaks. Another option is to ask for just one musician, perhaps the pianist, to play during breaks, such as during meal service when you want the music to be more sedate.

Confirm with the bandleader that once they are playing, there will be no downtime. A poorly organized band will sometimes pause after a song while they decide what to play next. No matter how short that pause is, guests will think the set is over, and within moments the energy will plummet and the dance floor will begin to empty.

With wedding dinners of the past, the entire meal was served before dancing. Now, it is fun to intersperse courses with short dance sets. With a multicourse dinner, you might serve the first and second courses, then have the band play some great dance music for a twenty-minute set. More dancing might occur after the main course. How you schedule the dancing is up to you, but be sure to communicate the plan to both the band and the caterer ahead of time. If you do want to break up your meal service with a few dance sets, always serve at least two courses before breaking for a dance set, in order to foster good conversation and create interaction at the tables.

For speeches and toasts, the bandleader can help by taking the music down in volume, getting the guests' attention, and introducing the first speaker. During the speeches, there should be no meal service or music. Determine in advance who wants to speak and ask them to keep their speeches to one to two minutes. Add them to the schedule with agreed-upon times. Short, sweet, and witty is the key to a successful wedding speech. For the same reason, try to limit the number of friends who speak. The best place for all the long, impromptu speeches is the night before, at the rehearsal dinner.

THE FINALE

It is important to plan the end of your celebration and be sure the party's finale is included in the schedule of events. Plan the time that the bartender will announce last call and the band will play their last song. To give your party a gentle finish, make sure that recorded background music continues to play after the band has stopped playing and they are breaking down their equipment.

Always end on a high note! The bouquet toss is traditionally done at the peak of the party, and can be a great send-off for the newlyweds. Arranging for a unique mode of transportation to whisk off the bride and groom makes a wonderful climax to a wedding celebration. Perhaps a vintage automobile might be rented for the occasion, with driver if you like. The arrival of a horse-driven carriage to transport the bride and groom to a nearby destination works equally well for a wedding on a farm or a wedding in Manhattan, where the carriage might wind through Central Park before arriving at the couple's hotel.

At one wedding that took place on a seaside estate in Miami, the bridal couple planned a honeymoon cruise on a boat departing the evening of their noontime wedding. As the bride and groom were mingling with guests after a sumptuous wedding luncheon under a canopy, the noise of a fast boat became audible. Within a minute, guests could make out the sleek profile of a vintage wooden cigarette boat heading toward the dock of the estate. With a flourish, the boat docked and the skipper made it fast. As guests gathered on the seawall, the bride and groom, still attired in wedding finery, boarded the boat and waved a fond good-bye to their guests. In seconds, they were a speck on the horizon as they sped toward their cruise ship in the harbor. Naturally, their luggage had been checked on board earlier that day.

In my native country, South Africa, there is a charming custom when the bride and groom are ready to leave the reception. The guests stand in two lines, lean forward, and form a long arch by linking hands with the person across from them. The bride and groom have to pass through this arch. As the newlyweds make their way, the guests sing a traditional song, "Wish Me Luck." It makes for a wonderful moment of community and is a fitting send-off after an evening's celebration.

LIVE MUSIC OPTIONS

There are many options for live music at your wedding reception. A basic dance band begins with a keyboard, bass, and percussion. A five-piece band might add an electric guitar and a saxophone, and is a good starting size for a typical wedding. Additional instruments may be added depending on the style of music that the band plays. Some bands specialize in one type of music; others are able to play a variety of musical styles, from swing to soft rock, rhythm and blues, and disco. If you want a "big band" sound, expect six to seven band members at least. A big band with a full brass section has up to thirteen horn players. Here are some options to consider:

Big band orchestra

Big band orchestra with a full brass section

Soul band

Rock band

Rhythm and blues band

Jazz band

Jazz trio or quartet

Marimba band (consisting of a keyboard, bass, drums, and marimba, a type of xylophone used in African music)

String trio or quartet

SET UP THE BAND EARLY

It is usually worth it to pay extra to get the band to set up early for a reception (prior to the cocktail hour). The band has to set up its equipment, make sure the on-site public address system is functioning properly, and do a thorough sound check. It is disturbing when the band arrives at the last minute, unloads equipment, and carries instruments and drums through the cocktail party.

A FEW RULES FOR A SUCCESSFUL PARTY

In your negotiations with vendors—the caterer, the photographer, the videographer, the band—be sure that several rules are clearly understood in advance. Those who are working should not drink alcohol during the party. Cigarette smoking, if permitted, should occur only in designated areas away from guests. Have the caterer feed the workers in a designated area with a prearranged menu.

You should ensure that food, nonalcoholic drinks, and plenty of water are available for the workers at your wedding, including those setting up the room. Assign a waiter to the band to bring drinks as required. The band can eat during a break in an area or table set apart from the guests.

There are so many creative ways to personalize your wedding. They range from the big ideas—holding your nuptials at a special place that has meaning to you and your groom—to the smallest details, like using your favorite flower in the groom's boutonniere. I hope this book provides you with an insight into some of the ways you can incorporate your personal style into your celebration. And I urge you at every opportunity in designing your wedding to take inspiration from your personality and that of your groom.

On your wedding day, you invite friends and family into your world on one of the most special days of your life. You and your groom create an environment for your guests that expresses who you are. From the flowers that decorate your ceremony site, to the food that you serve at your reception and the music that you use to express your feelings as you begin your new life together, every element should be chosen carefully.

Within these pages I have shared all my secrets to successful wedding celebrations, from a simple ceremony on the beach to an elaborate church wedding and formal dinner. The ideas in this book are guidelines to help stimulate your own creativity.

I understand how much work and planning is ahead of you. I often compare planning a wedding with producing a small movie. Actually, since everything at a wedding comes together at the same moment, it's more like working in live television! Like any major production, if you take an organized approach to the day and work to get everything possible done in advance, the wedding day will go much more smoothly and you can be a guest at your own party.

I am confident that using the approach that has worked for me over the years, you will be able to plan a celebration that is utterly yours from start to finish, and have a good time all the way. Relax and enjoy your wedding. Concentrate on savoring every precious moment of your special day.

I wish you my very best for a beautiful and fun-filled wedding and a long, healthy, and happy life together.

Colin Cowie

INDEX

254

CREDITS

Aika Aeshma: Page 63, bottom. Jack Caputo: Page 80, top; page 83, second down; page 106, center; page 107. Grey Crawford: Page 192. Curtis Dahl: Page 202, bottom left. Yitshak Dalal: Page 151, top. Alison Duke: Page 131; page 159; pages 160–161; pages 164–165; pages 176–177; page 180; page 183, top; page 186; page 198; page 199, center and bottom left and top right; page 201; page 202, top left; page 205; pages 212–213; page 215; page 220; pages 222–223; page 229; page 235, bottom left. Johnathan Farrer: Pages 43–44; page 45, center and bottom; page 170. Deborah Feingold: Page 7, page 11, pages 132–133; page 136, top; page 173; page 178; page 195; page 225. Nadine Froger: Page 50, bottom; pages 64–65, page 66, top; page 78, bottom; page 79, pages 84–85, page 87, bottom; pages 88–89; page 93, center; page 106, top; page 109; page 117; page 124, top; page 125; page 126, top; page 130, center; page 158; pages 162–163; pages 166–167; page 168, bottom left; pages 180–182; page 183, bottom; pages 184–185; pages 188–189; page 202, top middle, and center left; page 233, bottom center and bottom right; page 235 top right; page 236; page 251. Alec Hermer: Pages 12 –23; page 108; pages 111–116; page 118; pages 120–122; page 141, bottom; page 144, center and bottom; page 150;   page 172; page 179; page 187; page 190; page 193; page 196, bottom; page 199, top left; page 208; page 214; page 217; page 232; page 233, bottom left, page 234. Beth Herzhaft: Page 42; page 45, top; pages 47–49; pages 51–59, pages 68–77, page 78, top and center; page 80, center and bottom; pages 81–82, page 83, top, third down, and bottom; pages 96–102; page 126, bottom left; page 130; bottom; pages 138–139; page 144, top; page 149; page 151; page 156, second down; page 157; page 175; page 183, center; page 193; page 196, top; page 200; page 202, bottom right; page 218; page 233, top left,middle center, and middle right, page 235, top left; page 238; page 249; page 255. Leslie Holtz: Page168, top left and spread; page 169. Jono and Gorman: Page 154. Bart Kressa: Page 156, bottom; page 174. Judy Lawne: Page 231; pages 246–247. Brian Miller: Pages 210–211. Michelle Patter: Page 126, bottom right; page 171; page 191. Jean Jacques Pochet: Page 239. Denis Reggie: Page 86; page 87, top; pages 90–92, page 93, top, and bottom; pages 94–95; page 248. Raphael Reisman: Page 24, bottom; page 25, page 28, top; pages 29–31; page 50, top; pages 104–105; page 124, top; page 136, bottom; page 140; page 156, third down; pages 226–227. Lisa Romerian: Page 62, right bottom. Lee Salem: Page 152, top. Jasper Sky: Page 119. Baron Erik Spafford: Page 141; page 142; page 197. Timothy Teague: Page 24, top; pages 26–27; page 28, bottom; pages 33–41; pages 60–61; page 62, left top and left bottom; page 63, top; page 66, bottom; page 67; page 130, top; page 135; page 141, top; page 152, top; page 155; page 156, top; page 194; page 196, center; page 203; page 206.

Colin Cowie designs and produces parties around the world. Colin also lectures on entertaining, wedding planning, and interior design. This book is one in a series of books Colin will be authoring for Little, Brown and Company. Colin can be contacted at:
Colin Cowie Lifestyle, P.O.Box 480228, Los Angeles, CA 90048, telephone 213 462 7183.